VeriSM™ - Foundation Courseware

VeriSM™

Foundation Courseware

Colophon

Title:	VeriSM™ - Foundation Courseware
Authors:	Helen Morris & Liz Gallacher
Courseware reviewers:	Ademar Luccio
	Huub Commandeur
	Jaakko kuosmanen
	Jukka Tenkamaa
	Jeferson D'Addario
	Krzysztof Politowicz
	Kristian Spilhaug
	Marcos Sabino Gomes
	Martin Altermate
	Martin Cross
	Suzanne Van Hove
	Richard de Boer
	Jaap Germans
	Vincent Douhairie
	Ton Vromans
Cover illustration:	Frank van Driel, www.frankvandriel.com
Publisher:	Van Haren Publishing, Zaltbommel, www.vanharen.net
Design and Layout:	Coco Bookmedia, Amersfoort – NL
NUR code:	981 / 123
ISBN Hard copy:	978 94 018 262 8
ISBN eBook:	978 94 018 063 5
Edition:	First edition, first impression, January 2018
Copyright:	© Van Haren Publishing, 2018

About the Courseware

The Courseware was created by experts from the industry who served as the author(s) for this publication. The input for the material is based on existing publications and the experience and expertise of the author(s). The material has been revised by trainers who also have experience working with the material. Close attention was also paid to the key learning points to ensure what needs to be mastered.

The objective of the courseware is to provide maximum support to the trainer and to the student , during his or her training. The material has a modular structure and according to the author(s) has the highest success rate should the student opt for examination. The Courseware is also accredited for this reason, wherever applicable.

In order to satisfy the requirements for accreditation the material must meet certain quality standards. The structure, the use of certain terms, diagrams and references are all part of this accreditation. Additionally, the material must be made available to each student in order to obtain full accreditation. To optimally support the trainer and the participant of the training assignments, practice exams and results are provided with the material.

Direct reference to advised literature is also regularly covered in the sheets so that students can find additional information concerning a particular topic. The decision to leave out notes pages from the Courseware was to encourage students to take notes throughout the material.

Although the courseware is complete, the possibility that the trainer deviates from the structure of the sheets or chooses to not refer to all the sheets or commands does exist. The student always has the possibility to cover these topics and go through them on their own time. It is recommended to follow the structure of the courseware and publications for maximum exam preparation.

The courseware and the recommended literature are the perfect combination to learn and understand the theory.

Table of Content

This number is a reference to the sheet number

Agenda

VeriSM Foundation

Day 1		Day 2	
09:00 – 09:30	Introduction	09:00 – 10:00	**Module 4:** The VeriSM™ model
09:30 – 10:45	**Module 1:** The Service Organization	10:00 – 10:45	**Module 5:** Progressive practices
10:45 – 11:00	Break	10:45 – 11:00	Break
11:00 – 11:40	**Module 2:** Service culture	11:00 – 12:45	**Module 5:** Progressive practices
11:40 – 12:00	**Module 3:** People and organizational structure	12:45 – 13:15	Lunch
12:00 – 12:30	Lunch	13:15 – 14:30	**Module 6:** Innovative technologies
12:30 – 14:45	**Module 3:** People and organizational structure	14:30 – 14:45	Break
14:45 – 15:00	Break	14:45 – 15:05	**Module 7:** Getting started
15:00 – 17:00	**Module 4:** The VeriSM™ model	15:05 – 17:00	**Exam** (prep and 60 min duration)

VeriSM Essential

Day 1	
09:00 – 09:30	Introduction
09:30 – 10:30	**Module 1:** The Service Organization
10:30 – 10:45	Break
10:45 – 11:25	**Module 2:** Service culture
11:25 – 13:00	**Module 3:** People and organizational structure
13:00 – 13:30	Lunch
13:30 – 14:45	**Module 4:** The VeriSM™ model
14:45 – 15:00	Break
15:00 – 16:15	**Module 4:** The VeriSM™ model
16:15 – 17:00	**Exam** (prep and 30 min duration)

VeriSM Plus

Day 1	
09:00 – 09:30	Introduction
09:30 – 09:50	**Module 1:** The Service Organization
09:50 – 10:55	**Module 3:** People and organizational structure
10:55 – 11:10	Break
11:10 – 12:30	**Module 4:** The VeriSM™ model
12:30 – 13:00	Lunch
13:00 – 14:45	**Module 5:** Progressive practices
14:45 – 15:00	Break
15:00 – 15:45	**Module 6:** Innovative technologies
15:45 – 16:15	**Module 7:** Getting started
16:15 – 17:00	**Exam** (prep and 30 min duration)

VERISM™ SERVICE MANAGEMENT FOUNDATION

Introduction

- Let's meet & Goals
- Terms
- Program

VeriSM™ – Foundation Courseware

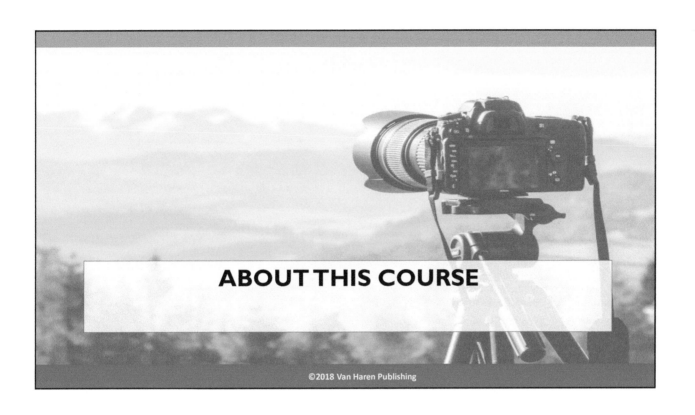

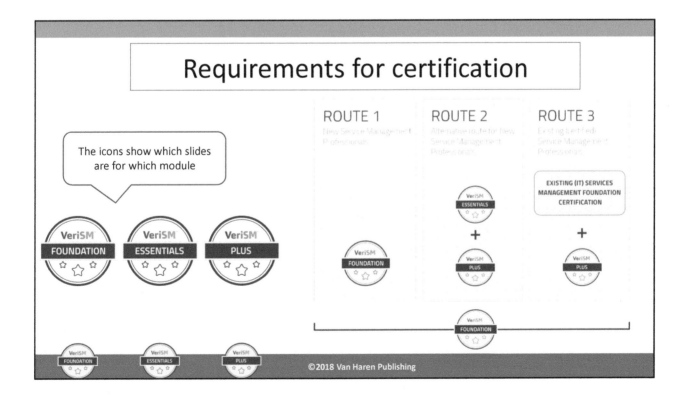

Contents

Program VeriSM Foundation

Day 1		Day 2	
09:00 – 9:30	Introduction	09:00 – 10:00	Module 4: VeriSM model
09:30 – 10:45	Module 1: Service Organization	10:00 – 10:45	Module 5: Progressive practices
10:45 – 11:00	Break	10:45 – 11:00	Break
11:00 – 11:40	Module 2: Service Culture	11:00 – 12:45	Module 5: Progressive practices
11:40 – 12:00	Module 3: People and organizational structure	12:45 – 13:15	Lunch
12:00 – 12:30	Lunch	13:15 – 14:30	Module 6: Innovative technologies
12:30 – 13:45	Module 3: People and organizational structure	14:30 – 14:45	Break
13:45 – 14:45	Module 4: VeriSM Model	14.45 – 15:05	Module 7: Getting started
14:45 – 15:00	Break	15:05 – 17:00	Exam (prep and 60 min duration)
15.00 – 17.00	Module 4: VeriSM model		

©2018 Van Haren Publishing

Contents

Program VeriSM Essential

Day 1

09:00 – 09:30	Introduction	13.30 – 14.45	Module 4: VeriSM model
09:30 – 10:30	Module 1: Service Organization	14:45 – 15:00	Break
10:30 – 10:45	Break	15:00 – 16:15	Module 4: VeriSM model
10:45 – 11:25	Module 2: Service Culture	16:15 – 17:00	Exam (prep and 30 min duration)
11:25 – 13:00	Module 3: People and organizational structure		
13.00 - 13:30	Lunch		

©2018 Van Haren Publishing

| Contents | **Program VeriSM Plus** |

Day 1

09:00 – 9:30	Introduction		13:00 – 14:45	Module 5: Progressive practices
09:30 – 09:50	Module 1: Service Organization		14:45 – 15:00	Break
09:50 – 10:55	Module 3: People and organizational structure		15:00 – 15:45	Module 6: Innovative practices
10:55 – 11:10	Break		15:45 – 16:15	Module 7: Getting started
11:10 – 12:30	Module 4: VeriSM model		16:15 - 17:00	Exam (prep and 30 min duration)
12:30 – 13:00	Lunch			

Here is the link from the slide to the theory in the book, with the number of the chapter or the paragraph (§) and possibly the name of the subtitle in the book

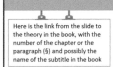

Literature

Foundation Study Guide

Courseware

Trainer slides
(Included in Courseware)

The figure numbers in the courseware correspond with the Body of knowledge:
'VeriSM™ - A service management approach for the digital age'

Scope of the Course

This certification includes the following topics:

1. The Service Organization
2. Service culture
3. People and organizational structure
4. The VeriSM™ model
5. Progressive practices
6. Innovative technologies
7. Getting started

See Syllabus
§ 1

Exam specifications

- VeriSM™ Foundation
- Examination type: Computer-based or paper-based multiple-choice questions
- Number of questions: 40
- Pass mark: 65% (26 out of 40)
- Open book/notes: No
- Electronic equipment/aides permitted: No
- Time allowed for examination: 60 minutes

See Syllabus § 2

Exam requirements

Certification requirement	Exam specification	Foundation
1. The Service Organization	1.1 Organizational context	2,5%
	1.2 Organizational governance	2,5%
	1.3 Digital transformation	5%
2. Service culture	2.1 Service culture	5%
3. People and organizational structure	3.1 Organization structure	10%
	3.2 Service Management challenges	10%
4. The VeriSM™ model	4.1 The VeriSM™ model	25%
	4.2 Adapting the VeriSM™ model	7,5%
5. Progressive practices	5.1 Progressive practices	20%
6. Innovative technologies	6.1 Impact of technology	10%
7. Getting started	7.1 Getting started	2,5%

©2018 Van Haren Publishing

©2018 Van Haren Publishing

VeriSM™ – Foundation Courseware

©2018 Van Haren Publishing

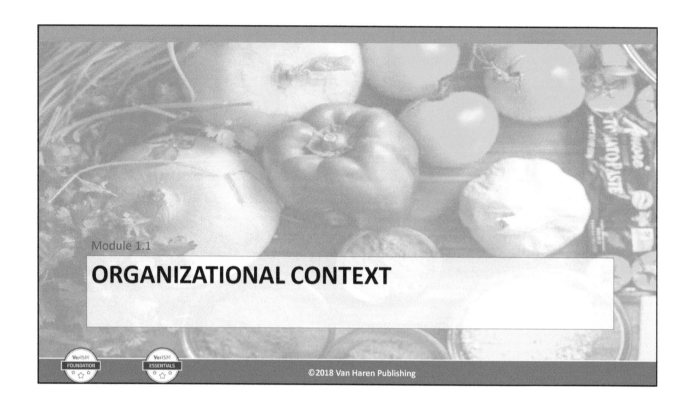

Module 1.1
ORGANIZATIONAL CONTEXT

---

§ 2.2

Organizational Context

Definition: Organization

"An organization is an official group of people, for example, a political party, a charity, or a club"

Types of organization:

- Private sector
- Public sector organizations
- Voluntary sector or charity organizations
- Non-profit organization
- Third sector

VeriSM™ – Foundation Courseware

§ 2.2.2

Key Terms

Definition: Consumer

"A consumer is a person who buys things or uses services."

- Service management uses various terms:
  - Client, customer, user or consumer
  - Customers pay for and define services; users receive services provided
- VeriSM uses "consumer" to include:
  - Clients, customers and users

§ 2.2.3

Key Terms

Definition: Asset

"An asset is anything that is useful or valuable within a product or service."
- Assets should be used to meet agreed consumer needs

Definition: Capability

"The ability or the qualities that are necessary to do something."
- A capability is not always a discrete team
- Examples include: Human resources; Finance; Marketing; Sales; Customer service; Information technology

§ 2.2.4 — Organizational Focus

- All organizational capabilities will be involved in digital service provision
- Effective service providers will focus on an outcome for their consumer

Definition: Outcome

"The end result of a consumer interacting with a product or service"

- An output focuses on a physical deliverable
- The service provider focus is on the overall experience for the consumer

§ 2.2.4 — Organization is a Service Provider

The Organization
is a Service Provider

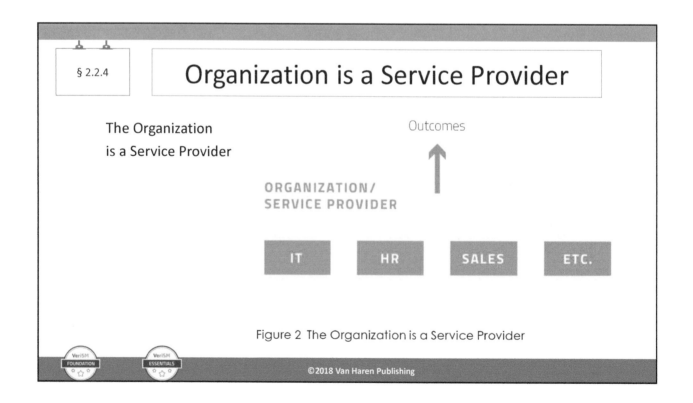

Figure 2 The Organization is a Service Provider

VeriSM™ – Foundation Courseware

§ 2.2.4

Good Service Provider

What makes a 'good' service provider organization? We need to understand:

- Consumers – where are they?
- Competition – who are the competitors?
- Structure – what is the organizational structure?
- Consumer culture – behaviors and local customs affect business
- Laws and regulations – is there any specific governance?
- Challenges – what challenges is the organization facing?

---

§ 2.2.5

Optimizing Organizational Interactions

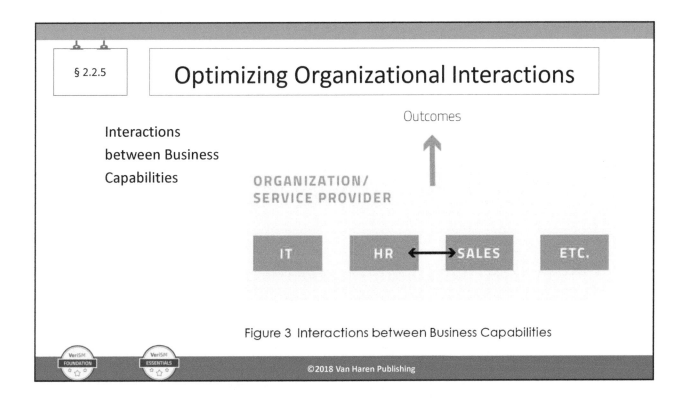

Interactions between Business Capabilities

Figure 3 Interactions between Business Capabilities

---

§ 2.2.6 — Shadow Behavior

- Shadow behavior is common in many organizations, described as:
  - *"Systems, processes, solutions and decisions implemented and used inside organizations without explicit organizational approval or service delivery consideration."*
  - Shadow IT refers to a system purchased without IT knowledge, but they are expected to provide support for it
- Shadow behavior is not restricted to the IT department
- To overcome and break down consumer and service provider barriers
  - Encourage an holistic approach to communication, collaboration, and shared mindset

§ 2.3

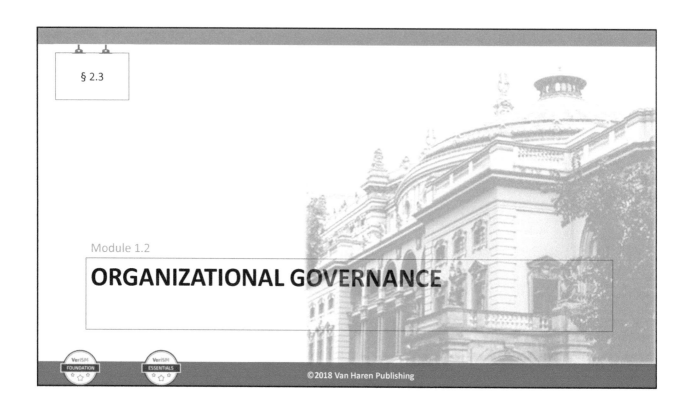

Module 1.2

ORGANIZATIONAL GOVERNANCE

§ 2.3 Organizational Governance

- Organizations need to have rules and guidelines about the way they work
  - This is specific to each organization
  - A set of governing principles, policies, metrics
- Governance principles cascade throughout the organizational capabilities
- Governance and management
  - Governance provides vision
  - Management makes decisions to fulfill the vision

---

§ 2.3.1 Organizational Governance

Governance:
- Evaluate,
- Direct,
- Monitor.

Management Activities

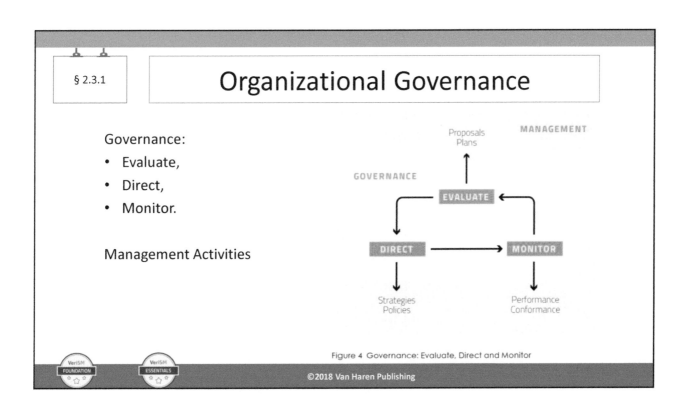

Figure 4 Governance: Evaluate, Direct and Monitor

---

§ 2.3.1

Governance Principles

Typical governance practices and principles include:

- Create and maintain the governance framework – define the structures, principles and practices based on the organization's goals and objectives (mission/vision).

- Ensure the value proposition – link the outcomes of the products and services to the achievement of organizational objectives."

- Optimize risks – define organizational risk tolerance and ensure it is understood, communicated and managed.

- Optimize capabilities – ensure there are sufficient resources (people, process, technology) to support the achievement of organizational objectives.

©2018 Van Haren Publishing

---

§ 2.3.2

Governance Flow

The Governance Flow

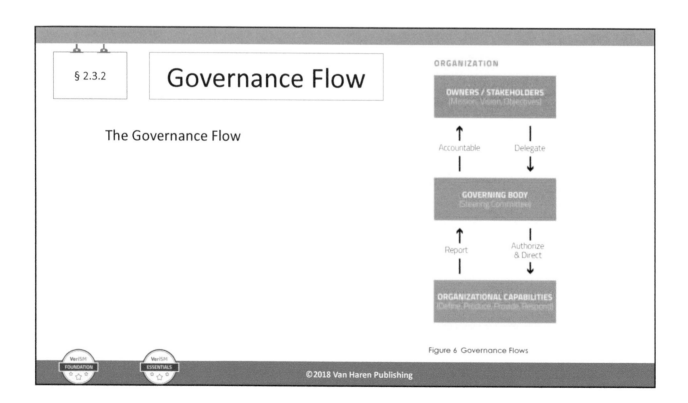

Figure 6 Governance Flows

©2018 Van Haren Publishing

§ 2.3.3

Governance Principles

Planning activities triggered by governance principles:

- Strategic planning
  - covers the direction of organization.
- Tactical planning
  - covers the 'where and how', typically looking forward for nine to eighteen months.
- Operational planning
  - covers the 'what', requiring individual and specific results.

©2018 Van Haren Publishing

Module 1.3

DIGITAL TRANSFORMATION

©2018 Van Haren Publishing

---

§ 2.4

Digital Transformation

Definition: Digital Transformation

"Digital transformation refers to the changes associated with the application of digital technologies across all areas of an organization, from sales to marketing, products, services and new business models"

Digital transformation is *"the rethinking, the reimagining of a business in more digital terms…It's fundamentally looking at delivery channels, operations, marketing and sales and customer care - all business models and rethinking how that might be packaged as new digital products and services, all delivered using digital first as the way business gets done."*

Dion Hinchcliffe

§ 2.4.1 / 2.4.2

Digital Transformation

- Transformation is driven both internally and externally
  - Organizations can exploit new technologies internally, and externally by the market
- Digital optimization:
  - Changing the use of technology to reach new markets, optimize operations
- Digital disruption:
  - Technology is used to radically change the operating performance of an organization
  - Technology is used to radically extend the reach of the organization to new customers and markets
  - Technology is used to radically seize customers or win new customers from competitors

Service Management & Digital Transformation

§ 2.4.3

- Service management needs to respond to digital transformation
  - Adopt more agile thinking
  - Technology is everywhere and services from anywhere
- IT capabilities must work within other organizational capabilities to deliver products and services
- Service management coordinates capabilities
  - 'Inside-out' to 'outside-in' (customer oriented, rather than business dictated)
  - Consider:
    - *How does the organization enable and deliver value?*
    - *What are the supply chains within the organization that deliver value?*
    - *How do the individual capabilities contribute to or support the supply chains to deliver value?*

©2018 Van Haren Publishing

Quiz questions

Module 1

- What is a "consumer"?

a) A person who provides services

b) An organization that delivers a product

c) A person who buys things or uses services

d) An organization who works with others to deliver services

©2018 Van Haren Publishing

| Module 1 | Quiz questions |

- What is a "consumer"?

a) A person who provides services
b) An organization that delivers a product
c) A person who buys things or uses services
d) An organization who works with others to deliver services

©2018 Van Haren Publishing

| Module 1 | Quiz questions |

- What are the three elements of governance?

a) Evaluate, direct and monitor
b) Evaluate, deliver and measure
c) Review, deliver and monitor
d) Audit, direct and measure

©2018 Van Haren Publishing

VeriSM™ – Foundation Courseware

©2018 Van Haren Publishing

Module 1

Quiz questions

- What are the three elements of governance?

a) Evaluate, direct and monitor
b) Evaluate, deliver and measure
c) Review, deliver and monitor
d) Audit, direct and measure

©2018 Van Haren Publishing

Module 1

Quiz questions

- How does digital transformation refer to consumer thinking?

a) 'Outside-in' to 'Inside-out'
b) Provider centric
c) Supplier centric
d) 'Inside-out' to 'Outside-in'

©2018 Van Haren Publishing

Quiz questions

- How does digital transformation refer to consumer thinking?

a) 'Outside-in' to 'Inside-out'
b) Provider centric
c) Supplier centric
d) 'Inside-out' to 'Outside-in'

MODULE 2: SERVICE CULTURE

VeriSM™ – Foundation Courseware

Module 2.1

SERVICE CULTURE

---

§ 3.1

Service Culture

Definition: Service Culture

- A service culture exists when an organization's staff, products, services and business processes are developed with a focus on the end consumer or customer.
- Quality of service:
  - How service is provided?
  - What is provided?
- Service culture is the responsibility of everyone within the organization
  - Led from the top

VeriSM™ – Foundation Courseware

§ 3.2

Service Culture

Key Elements:

- Adaptability / flexibility
  - Variations to a standard offering
- Focus on service quality in addition to product quality
  - Poor service experience with a good product will impact the consumer
- Management of expectations
  - Setting consumer expectations will affect the satisfaction rating
- Consumer focus
  - staff in the service provider organization is either serving consumers directly, or enabling others to serve consumers

§ 3.2.4

Service Culture: E^{10}

Element	Includes
Empathy	Putting yourself in the consumer's position.
Excellence	Exceeding consumer expectations.
Empowerment	Allowing staff to act in the consumer's interests.
Engagement	Appearing approachable and personable.
Easy to do business with	Efficient, easy to contact.
Everyone	All staff understand their contribution to the whole.
Environment	Culture of the organization.
Experience	The reality of the product or service matches what was promised.
Encouragement	Service provider staff get recognition and rewards.
Effective	The service provider delivers what was promised, when it was promised.

§ 3.3 — Create a Service Culture

- Senior management create a service culture through:
  - Empowerment
  - Motivation
  - Behavior
  - Management responsibility
  - Contribution
  - Measuring culture
  - Reward and recognition

Module 2 — Quiz questions

- How does VeriSM refer to the elements of a well developed service culture?

a) E^1

b) E^5

c) E^7

d) E^{10}

Quiz questions

- How does VeriSM refer to the elements of a well developed service culture?

a) E^1

b) E^5

c) E^7

d) E^{10}

Quiz questions

- What are some of the key elements identified as part of a service culture?
1. Adaptability / flexibility
2. Consumer focus
3. Meeting ROI targets
4. Management of expectations

a) 1, 3 & 4

b) 1, 2 & 4

c) 2, 3 & 4

d) 1, 2 & 3

Module 2	Quiz questions

- What are some of the key elements identified as part of a service culture?
1. Adaptability / flexibility
2. Consumer focus
3. Meeting ROI targets
4. Management of expectations

a) 1, 3 & 4
b) 1, 2 & 4
c) 2, 3 & 4
d) 1, 2 & 3

©2018 Van Haren Publishing

Module 2	Quiz questions

- Who is responsible for service culture in an organization?

a) Everyone in the organization
b) Only the service provider
c) Only the consumer of the organization
d) The service owner in the organization

©2018 Van Haren Publishing

Module 2

Quiz questions

- Who is responsible for service culture in an organization?

a) Everyone in the organization
b) Only the service provider
c) Only the consumer of the organization
d) The service owner in the organization

VeriSM™

MODULE 3: PEOPLE AND ORGANIZATIONAL STRUCTURE

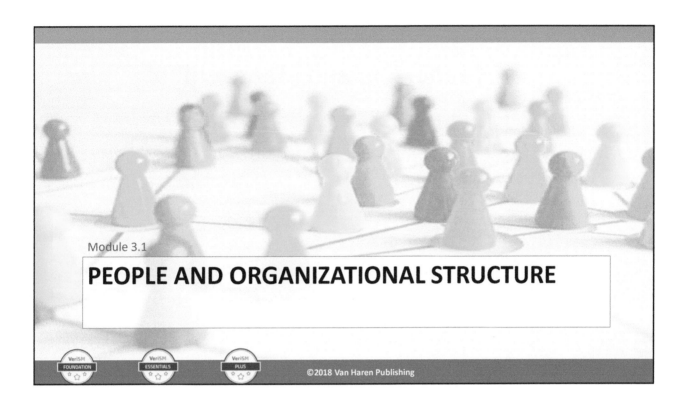

Module 3.1

PEOPLE AND ORGANIZATIONAL STRUCTURE

---

§ 4.2

Relationship Management

- Relationship management covers the management of individuals and teams
- All organizations have leaders and managers

Leaders	Managers
▪ Set goals and direction;	▪ Resource-oriented;
▪ Challenge the norm;	▪ Plan, budget and organize;
▪ Look for new ways to excel;	▪ Maintain the status quo;
▪ Motivate, empower and inspire.	▪ Minimize risk;
	▪ Focus on results.

VeriSM™ – Foundation Courseware

§ 4.2

Leadership and Management

The Relationship
of Leadership
and Management

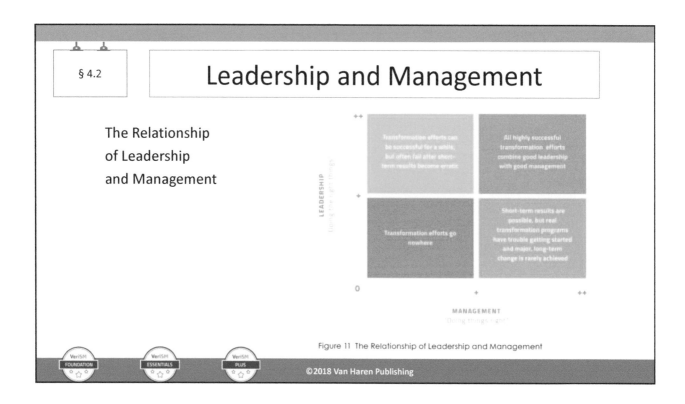

Figure 11 The Relationship of Leadership and Management

---

§ 4.2

Leaders and Managers

- Service providers need leaders and managers
  - Leaders are found throughout the hierarchy of an organization
- Leaders
  - Exploit organizational capabilities to deliver products or services
  - Use capabilities to differentiate the service provider from competitors
- Managers
  - Oversee activities that produce and support the services
  - Ensure activities stay within the governance and service management principles
- Leaders and managers need to manage people
  - Respond appropriately to emotional needs of staff

§ 4.4 Competence vs. Competencies

Definition: Competence

"a cluster of related abilities, commitments, knowledge and skills that enable a person...to act effectively in a job or situation. Competence indicates sufficiency of knowledge and skills that enable someone to act in a wide variety of situations. Because each level of responsibility has its own requirements, competence can occur in any period of a person's life or at any stage of his or her career."

- What is the difference between competences and competencies?
  - Competence is the capability to carry out a defined function effectively.
  - Competency is the description of the knowledge, skills, experience and attributes necessary to carry out a defined function effectively.
- In short, a competence's focus is on the *what* and the competency's focus is on the *how*.

§ 4.3 Emotional Intelligence

- Leaders and managers require Emotional Intelligence (EQ)
- Emotional Intelligence has two competences, four skills

Personal competence	Social competence
Self-awareness	Social awareness
Self-management	Relationship management

- EQ is more important than IQ when achieving goals
- EQ can be developed to improve individual performance

§ 4.4

Competence Frameworks

- Leaders and managers within each organizational capability must develop the appropriate competencies to delivery quality services
- Internationally recognized IT competence frameworks include:
  - The European e-Competence Framework (e-CF)
  - Skills Framework for the Information Age (SFIA)

---

§ 4.4

Gartner EXP Competencies

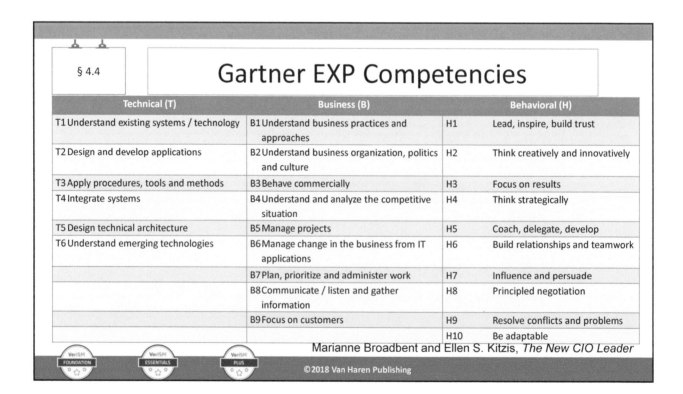

Technical (T)	Business (B)		Behavioral (H)	
T1 Understand existing systems / technology	B1 Understand business practices and approaches	H1	Lead, inspire, build trust	
T2 Design and develop applications	B2 Understand business organization, politics and culture	H2	Think creatively and innovatively	
T3 Apply procedures, tools and methods	B3 Behave commercially	H3	Focus on results	
T4 Integrate systems	B4 Understand and analyze the competitive situation	H4	Think strategically	
T5 Design technical architecture	B5 Manage projects	H5	Coach, delegate, develop	
T6 Understand emerging technologies	B6 Manage change in the business from IT applications	H6	Build relationships and teamwork	
	B7 Plan, prioritize and administer work	H7	Influence and persuade	
	B8 Communicate / listen and gather information	H8	Principled negotiation	
	B9 Focus on customers	H9	Resolve conflicts and problems	
		H10	Be adaptable	

Marianne Broadbent and Ellen S. Kitzis, *The New CIO Leader*

VeriSM™ – Foundation Courseware

§ 4.1.1   T-shaped Professional

- The skills required to be a T-shaped professional are:
  - In depth knowledge of at least one area of a service system
  - Generalist knowledge across the organization as a whole, technology, people and shared information

Figure 14 The T-Shaped Professional

©2018 Van Haren Publishing

---

§ 4.5   What is a Profession?

- Established via specialized training, providing objective advice and service
  - Medicine, law and divinity
  - Nursing, civil engineering, architecture, accounting, social work, etc.
- Professions are important
  - Code of Ethics
- Is IT a profession?

©2018 Van Haren Publishing

VeriSM™ – Foundation Courseware

©2018 Van Haren Publishing

§ 4.5   Elements of a Profession

Required element	Description
Body of Knowledge	Supplemented with specific knowledge and skills associated with the specialism; the BoK is continuously maintained and updated.
Proven experience	Practical experience of the competence being exercised. Before gaining a license or certification, a documented work program must be completed.
Certification / licensing	Proof of competence via an exam; licensing is similar but managed at a government level and has legal ramifications; usually some form of re-certification is mandatory
Continuing education / professional development	Required ongoing learning to ensure the professional maintains the necessary skills and knowledge (most common in rapidly changing professions, e.g., medicine).
Professional societies	A community of like-minded individuals who put the professional standards above their self-interest; defines certification criteria, accreditation standards
Code of ethics	Frames the boundaries of relationships (what they do and what they should do) with customers, colleagues and society (integrity, confidentiality, competence).
Accountability	Personal responsibility for the quality and effectiveness of work
Earns a living	A significant proportion of one's work activities relate to the practice of the specialism

©2018 Van Haren Publishing

---

§ 4.6   Service Management and Teams

- Service management is rarely achieved by an individual
- Teams are a vital part of the success of service management

Definition: Team

"A small number of people with complementary skills who are committed to a common purpose, performance goals, and approach for which they hold themselves mutually accountable."

- To be successful and develop, deliver and support products and services, it is necessary to have a cohesive team.

©2018 Van Haren Publishing

---

§ 4.6.1 Team Development

Stage	Description	Leadership strategy	Keys to Success
Forming	The group focuses on getting to know each other and understand the purpose of the team.	Coordination	Pick a team with a purpose in mind Facilitate development of goals for individuals and the team;
Storming	Disagreements occur around the mission, vision and problem-solving approach, which stem from the team continuing to try to understand each other.	Coach	Clarify the assignment, as needed; Act as a resource; Listen and support; build trust.
Norming	The group consciously or unconsciously has accepted the working relationships and group norms.	Empower	Ask for updates; check progress; Allow leadership to transfer to the team.
Performing	Relationships, team practices and its effectiveness are synced and the real work of the team is now progressing.	Empower	Check progress with periodic updates; Ensure transparency (no silos within the team and other parties).
Adjourning	Group tasks are complete and the team disbands.	Support	Clearly end the team with a project review (success, improvements...) and/or celebration.

Bruce W. Tuckman, Developmental Sequence in Small Groups (1965)

©2018 Van Haren Publishing

---

§ 4.6.2 Building a Team

- Clarity
- Context
- Commitment
- Competence
- Charter
- Control

- Collaboration
- Communication
- Creativity
- Consequences
- Coordination
- Culture

Susan M. Heathfield *"12 tips for team building in the workplace"*

©2018 Van Haren Publishing

---

§ 4.6.4 Successful Team Behaviors

- Sharing
  - Freedom to challenge and support, achieve a shared goal
- Cooperation
  - Identify and exploit the individual strengths of the team
- Collaboration
  - Should be regularly reviewed, and encouraged as the normal practice
- Consensus decision-making
  - Requires an organization to provide opportunities for people to meet and discuss in a relaxed environment.

§ 4.6.4 Teamwork Culture

- Teamwork culture requires:
  - Clearly communicated goals and executive leadership teamwork examples;
  - Teamwork rewarded and recognized as an organizational value;
  - Performance measurement that emphasizes and value teamwork, with 360-degree feedback
  - Teams are successful when they have specific problems to solve, and have defined expectations and accountabilities.
  - Team building retreats often fail long term, as they do not relate to real world experience.
  - Team building is a daily challenge and needs to be driven by work activities.

Module 3.2

SERVICE MANAGEMENT CHALLENGES

---

§ 4.8

Relationship Management

- Describes how interactions between stakeholders take place
  - Organizations need a strategy for relationship management
  - Relationships with consumers, capabilities and suppliers
- People management is often harder than technology management
- Internal relationship management challenges include:
  - Silos and tribalism; virtual teams
- External relationship management challenges include:
  - Consumers; suppliers

---

§ 4.7.1 — Tribalism

- Managing teams can be challenging
- Teams have a shared identity
  - Common skills
  - Risk that the team becomes inward looking
  - Often known as 'a silo'
  - Known as tribalism

Definition: Tribalism

"Tribalism refers to the loyalties that people feel towards particular social groups and to the way these loyalties affect their behavior and their attitudes towards others"

§ 4.7.1 — Teams vs. Silos

Team	Silo / Tribal Culture
Common identity	Common identity
Shares information	Guards information
Sees the big picture (the forest)	Sees only their goal (their tree)
Networks	Withdraws
Us and them	Us versus Them
Collaborative	Controlling

§ 4.7.1 How to Overcome Silos / Tribalism

- The desired team behaviors can be encouraged by:
  - Clearly defining roles and goals for the team(s)
  - Sharing information on the organization's strategies and initiatives
  - Clearly prioritizing activities at the strategic level, to support prioritization within teams;
  - Empowering decision-making
  - Communicating with collaboration in mind

§ 4.7.2 Management of Virtual Teams

- Challenges of virtual teams:
  - Technological mobility enables staff to work from anywhere
  - Collaboration tools enable virtual team working and communication
  - Team members are not connected by location or time zone
- Successful management of virtual teams includes:
  - Face to face meeting early in team development, and repeated if possible
  - Clarification of tasks and how to complete them
  - Simplification of tasks, with specific assignment, and review
  - Communication, consistency of communication, regularity of communication
  - All meetings should have an agenda, a defined purpose for the meeting

VeriSM™ – Foundation Courseware

§ 4.8.1   Consumer Management

- Relationship management also covers consumer and supplier management
- Organizations need to adapt to the expectation of consumers
  - Digital services consumers may have little direct interaction
- Relationships with consumers need to cover:
  - Interactivity – does the organization provide an appropriate response to social media or chat capability with the consumer
  - Condensing communication – avoid communication overload through digital media
  - Personalization – can be powerful in communicating to consumers, based on automation and analytics
  - Transparency – relationships work best based on trust, and consumers can easily verify information presented by a service provider

§ 4.8.2   Supplier Management

- Supplier and contract management are part of relationship management
- Supplier contracts cannot be solely focused on financial benefits
- Key considerations include:
  - Understand the entire supply chain, can there be a partnership?
  - Accountability must rest with the commissioning organization
  - Measurement should be clear and agreed
  - Penalties and incentives should be balanced in a contract
  - How will change management be handled across the supply chain?
  - What continuity arrangements need to be in place?
  - Honesty and transparency should work both ways

§ 4.8.3

Expectation Management

Definition: Expectation management
> *"A formal process to continuously capture, document and maintain the content, dependencies and sureness of the expectations for persons participating in an interaction and to apply the information to make the interaction successful".*

- Managing expectations is a key part of relationship management
- Managing expectations can mitigate difficulties in managing relationships
- False expectations of high performance can be perceived as failure to deliver
  - Better to under-promise and over achieve
- Ensure exceeding expectation is cost justifiable, and does not set an unachievable precedent

---

§ 4.8.3

Key Elements to Manage Expectations

- Clarity
  - Organization and supplier must understand the requirements for delivery
  - Clarity requires boundaries and structure, what is in scope and what is not, how the work supports the organization
- Make no assumptions
  - Making assumptions carries additional risk
- Have a contingency plan
  - Risk assessment and management provides mitigation
  - Teams need to be prepared for all eventualities

Communication

§ 4.8.4

- Communication is fundamental to success in relationships
- Five components of communication:
  - Who is the sender of the message?
  - What is the context of the message?
  - Who is the receiver of the message?
  - What is the mechanism for delivery?
  - What is the message content?
- Good communication is dependent on these aspects being successful

Communication Planning

§ 4.8.4

- Good communication plans should include:
  - What is the scope – a specific task, or project?
  - Who is engaged in the communication?
  - What are the roles and responsibilities for the tasks?
  - Timing is critical; what are the timeframes?
  - What is the choice of delivery mechanism?
  - The expected results of the communication, and was it achieved?
  - What are the escalation paths for challenges to the communication?
  - When will regular reviews take place, to keep the plan relevant, as requirements will change over time

VeriSM™ – Foundation Courseware

§ 4.8.4

Supporting the Communication Plan

- A communication plan needs a framework to support it
  - Communication is two-way, providing a feedback loop
  - Collaboration tools and techniques track team engagement, with management support
  - Regular status meetings, starting with a kick-off, keep things on track

§ 4.9

Getting Buy-In within the Organization

- Organizational change is challenging
  - Change almost always takes longer and costs more than expected
  - Managing stakeholders is critical
  - People need to feel engaged for the change to be accepted
- Changing the way people engage in work is known as "cultural change"
  - Many practices support cultural change, providing structure, preparation, motivation and education
  - Without effect cultural change management there is a greater risk of failure of an initiative
- John Kotter's 8-step process of creating change
  - *Leading Change* (1996) and *Accelerate* (2014) Boston, MA: Harvard Business School Press

Kotter's 8-steps for Organizational Change

- Both *Leading Change* and *Accelerate* consider:
  - Complacency;
  - Lack of leadership;
  - Lack of vision;
  - Poor communication;
  - Lack of short-term wins;
  - Ending the effort too soon;
  - Lack of ongoing measurement
- Ignoring these errors will potentially lead to failures, wasted resources, lack of results and poor quality

---

Comparison of Kotter's Models

Step	Leading Change (1996)	Accelerate (2014)
1	Establish a sense of urgency – understand the market or competitive situation and discuss the implications or opportunities.	Create a sense of urgency – use opportunities that will appeal (emotionally and intellectually) to the volunteer army to urgently act.
2	Create a guiding coalition – put together a representative group that has the power to lead the change and can work as a team.	Build a guiding coalition – create the volunteer army with effective people who can guide, coordinate and communicate.
3	Develop a vision and strategy – a vision will help direct the effort and a strategy lays out the activities to achieve the vision.	Strategic vision and initiatives – well-designed and quickly executed activities that are targeted and coordinated help to turn the vision into reality.
4	Communicate the vision – constant communication via multiple methods of the vision is critical, as is the modelling of the behavior by the coalition.	Enlist a volunteer army – enthuse and drive change with significant numbers of actively engaged employees to a common purpose.

J. P. Kotter - Leading Change / Accelerate. Boston, MA: Harvard Business School Press

---

Comparison of Kotter's Models

Step	Leading Change (1996)	Accelerate (2014)
5	Empower action - eliminate obstacles, change systems/behaviors that undermine the vision and encourage risk-taking (non-traditional activities, ideas or actions).	Enable action by removing barriers – remove the inefficient processes or hierarchy to allow cross-organizational innovation.
6	Generate short-term wins – celebrate the small achievements and ensure the people who were behind the win are recognized.	Generate short-term wins – collect and categorize the short-term wins to show the achievement of tangible business results.
7	Consolidate gains and produce more change – use the success to create additional change in other systems, services, practices; reinvigorate the process for new projects.	Sustain acceleration – strategic adaptation to situations increases business gains and moves the organization closer to their vision.
8	Embed the change – measure new behaviors to ensure the change is now part of the corporate culture; continue to develop leaders and effective management practices.	Institute change – agility and speed is a business requirement; link new behaviors to the success of the organization.

Applying Kotter's Model

- Kotter – Leading Change or Accelerate
- Stages 1 – 4 are preparatory activities
- Stages 5 – 7 are used to introduce the new practices
- Stage 8 consolidates the change into organizational culture
- Each version of the eight steps encourages the stages to be active simultaneously or in parallel
  - All of the stages are completed
  - Without the first stages, there is no foundation
  - Without the middle stages there are no new practices
  - Without the last stage there is no long term outcome

Managing Stakeholders for Successful Organizational Change

Stakeholder Analysis

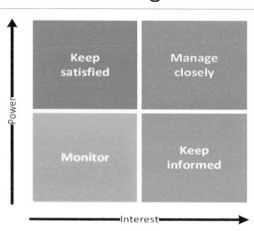

J. P. Kotter - Leading Change / Accelerate. Boston, MA: Harvard Business School Press

---

Stakeholder Management

- A cultural change requires a sponsor to act as champion for the change
  - Go-between for team and those impacted by the change
  - Stakeholder with engagement and responsibility
  - Must understand the role and skills required
- Sponsor is responsible for communication of benefits and drivers
  - Overcoming resistance
  - Mentoring and coaching for the team
- Three supporting plans
  - Communication plan (already reviewed)
  - Training plan documenting the skills for the change
  - Resistance management plan for addressing and mitigating any resistance

---

| Module 3 | Quiz questions |

- What are the two competences of Emotional Intelligence?

a) Performance competence and Social competence
b) Performance competence and Skill competence
c) Personal competence and Social competence
d) Personal competence and Skill competence

| Module 3 | Quiz questions |

- What are the two competences of Emotional Intelligence?

a) Performance competence and Social competence
b) Performance competence and Skill competence
c) Personal competence and Social competence
d) Personal competence and Skill competence

Module 3

Quiz questions

- Someone who has both a specialism and a broad generalist knowledge across the organization is known as what type of professional?

a) An I shaped professional
b) A Y shaped professional
c) A P shaped professional
d) A T shaped professional

©2018 Van Haren Publishing

Module 3

Quiz questions

- Someone who has both a specialism and a broad generalist knowledge across the organization is known as what type of professional?

a) An I shaped professional
b) A Y shaped professional
c) A P shaped professional
d) A T shaped professional

©2018 Van Haren Publishing

Module 3

Quiz questions

- Which of these best describes some of the competencies of a Leader?

a) Resource oriented; plan, budget and organize
b) Set goals and direction; motivate, empower and inspire
c) Plan, budget and organize; challenge the norm
d) Minimize risk; focus on results

Module 3

Quiz questions

- Which of these best describes some of the competencies of a Leader?

a) Resource oriented; plan, budget and organize
b) Set goals and direction; motivate, empower and inspire
c) Plan, budget and organize; challenge the norm
d) Minimize risk; focus on results

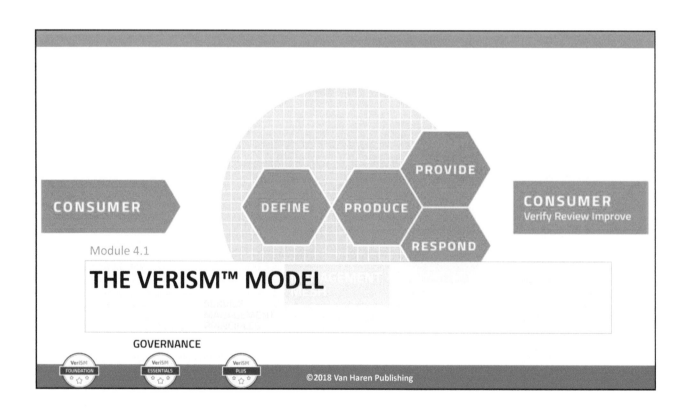

Module 4.1

THE VERISM™ MODEL

GOVERNANCE

VeriSM™ – Foundation Courseware

§ 5

Service Operating Model

Definition: Service management operating model

'A service management operating model is a visual representation showing how the organization will deliver on its strategy and provide value to its customers through products and services.'

- Service management operating model covers:
  - Definition, production and provision of products and services
  - Not prescriptive
  - Connected to organizational strategy
  - Operating model content and design is the result of strategy
  - Strategy may change due to the operating model

©2018 Van Haren Publishing

---

§ 5

Service Operating Model

- Every organization has an end-to-end operating model
  - Often not documented
  - Enables clarity and consistent working practices
- Operating models should be regularly reviewed
  - If required map future state, the target operating model
- Benefits of an operating model include:
  - Conformity, compliance and consistency
  - Optimized processes and resources, reducing redundancy and duplication
  - Improved decision-making
  - Reduced costs and increasing value

©2018 Van Haren Publishing

---

§ 5

Service Operating Model

- As the organization changes, the operating model will also change
- Regular assessment is required to ensure the model is still appropriate
- Assessment should include elements such as:
  - Is it fit for the organization's processes and requirements?
  - Is the documentation up to date?
  - Does the model address issues, risks and opportunities adequately?
  - Are strategic goals communicated to staff?
  - Is there a focus on ensuring performance is directed to organizational goals?
  - Is the model audited for compliance to any specific requirements?
  - How does the model compare to industry benchmarks?

©2018 Van Haren Publishing

§ 5.1

The VeriSM™ Model

- VeriSM operating model includes:
  - Governance and Service Management principles
    - Defined and communicated, only changed if the organizational requirement changes
  - Management Mesh
    - Allows for application of multiple management practices flexibly for services and products
- Characteristics of the model:
  - Not prescriptive, organization can use any management practices
  - Adopting the model allows:
    - Definition of governance requirements and service management principles
    - Creation of a Management Mesh
    - Management of the stages of a product or service from requirements definition to provision to the consumer and improvements, as needed

©2018 Van Haren Publishing

VeriSM™ – Foundation Courseware

©2018 Van Haren Publishing

The VeriSM™ Model

The VeriSM model

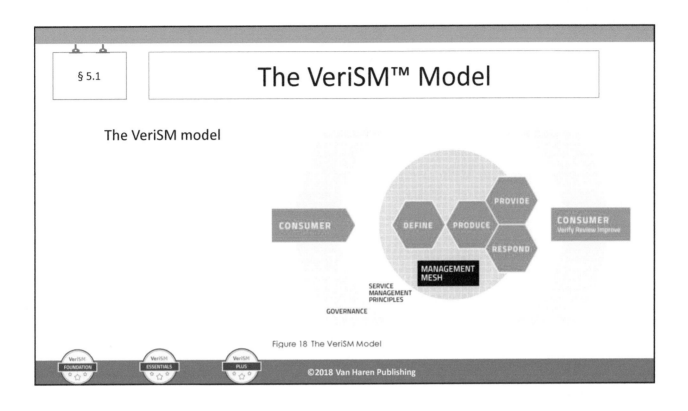

Figure 18 The VeriSM Model

©2018 Van Haren Publishing

Ch. 8

Governance

Governance

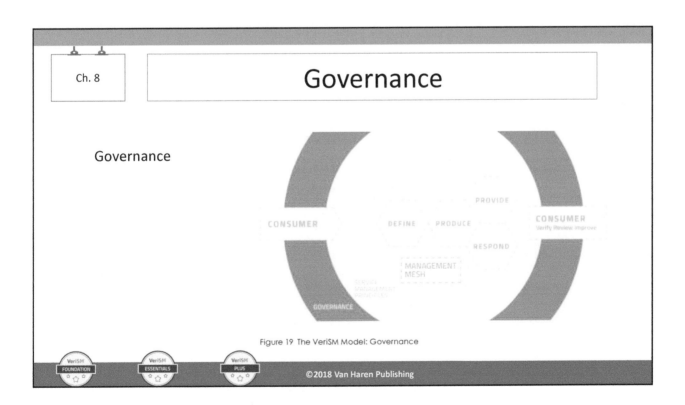

Figure 19 The VeriSM Model: Governance

©2018 Van Haren Publishing

---

§ 5.3

Governance

- Governance communicates the organization's strategic requirements
- Translates requirements into:
  - Object and goals (Direct activity)
  - Framework of reporting and audit (Evaluate and Monitor activities)
- Service management takes on the strategic requirements
  - Create service management principles
  - Shape the Management Mesh
- Governance
  - Applied throughout the capabilities for product and service development, production and provision

---

§ 5.3

Good Governance

- Examples of good governance:
  - Transparency
    - How decisions are made and by whom, visible to all staff
    - Appeals process to challenge decisions, organizationally specific
  - Accountability
    - Governing body accountable for its decisions
    - Accountable for outcomes associated with decisions
  - Responsiveness
    - Effectively balance competing requirements

VeriSM™ – Foundation Courseware

Good Governance

- Examples of good governance:
  - Effectiveness and efficiency
    - Use resources in the best possible way
  - Equitable and inclusive
    - All of the organizational members feel their interests have been considered in the decision-making process
  - Participatory
    - Anyone affected by or interested in a decision may participate in the decision-making process

---

Service Management Principles

Service
Management
Principles

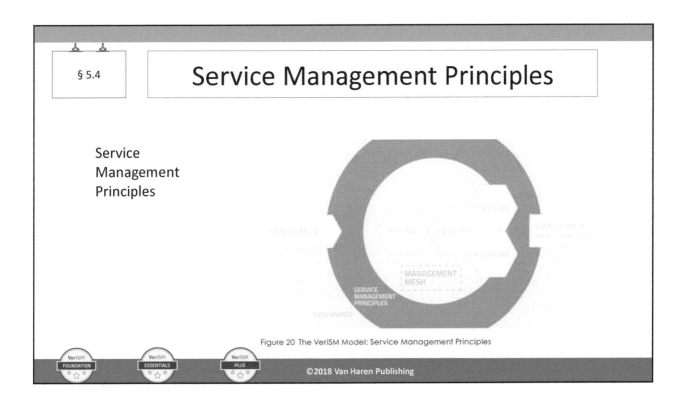

Figure 20 The VeriSM Model: Service Management Principles

§ 5.4

Service Management Principles

Definition: Service

"Fulfilment of a defined consumer need"

Definition: Service Management

"The management approach adopted by an organization to deliver value to consumers through quality products and services"

- Service management often perceived to be IT's responsibility
- VeriSM model defines service management principles at the organizational level
- Principles act as "guardrails" for product and service teams
- Allows and supports the use of different progressive management practices

©2018 Van Haren Publishing

§ 5.4

Service Management Principles

- Governance sets the boundaries for organizational management
- Management directs the organization to fulfil its objectives
- Management consists of many related elements, including:
  - Policies
  - Processes
  - Procedures
- VeriSM uses service management principles to define these elements
  - Applied across all products and services

©2018 Van Haren Publishing

VeriSM™ – Foundation Courseware

§ 5.2

VeriSM and Service Management

- Service management has historically been IT centric
- VeriSM recognize service management principles are applicable to the whole organization
- VeriSM redefines the term service provider
  - Entire organization is a service provider, providing service to its consumers
- All departments are capabilities
  - Capabilities are made up of people, knowledge, processes
  - Supports how an organization delivers action and outcomes meeting consumer needs
  - All capabilities are equal partners
  - Organizational capabilities should be assessed

©2018 Van Haren Publishing

---

§ 5.2.1

Benefits of Service Management

- Service management benefits include:
  - Understanding, meeting the needs, and managing expectations of the consumer
  - Ensuring an effective communications channel between the consumer and supplier
  - The provision and management of efficient, effective and economical services
  - Repeatable and scalable processes, meeting regulatory and compliance requirements
  - Measurable and consistent results with a focus on outcomes
  - The cost of delivery is in line with the benefits that result
  - A culture of continual improvement, ensuring that services provided remain aligned with the mission and vision of the organization.
  - Defined roles with assigned accountability and responsibility

©2018 Van Haren Publishing

---

§ 5.2.2 — Service Management Principles

- The principles will evolve into organizational policies:
  - Reputation
  - Commercial
  - Knowledge
  - Change
  - Asset and resource utilization
  - Finance
  - Quality
  - Risk
  - Security

§ 5.5 — Management Mesh

The Management Mesh

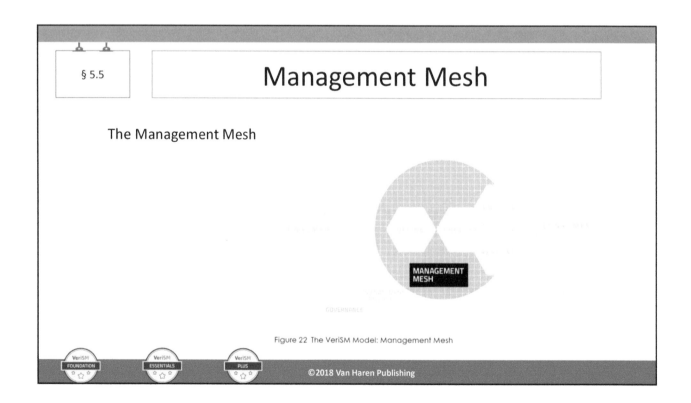

Figure 22 The VeriSM Model: Management Mesh

§ 5.5

Management Mesh

Structure

- Resources
- Emerging technologies
- Environment
- Management practices

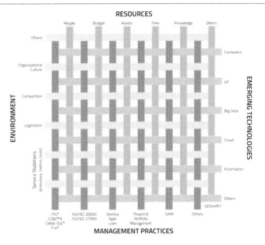

Figure 24 Possible Elements of the Management Mesh

---

§ 5.5

Management Mesh

- The Management Mesh consists of whichever practices are appropriate
- Flexibility is the essential characteristic
  - Organizations that focus on a single familiar approach may appear rigid
  - One practice may be more relevant than another for the organization
  - The Mesh can flex to accommodate this, without breaking
  - Ensures the organization delivers value to both the consumer and the provider
- Each organization's Mesh will be unique
  - Based on culture and capabilities, resources, environment, emerging technologies and management practices, simple or complex
  - Cannot be bought like a software tool
  - It is not a fixed design, it will evolve as required

Building the Mesh

Building the Mesh

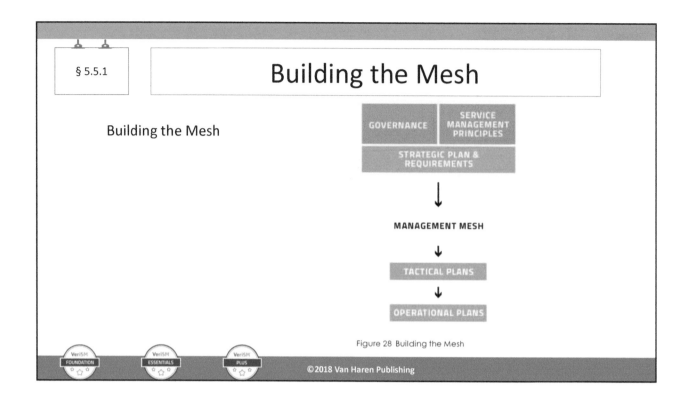

Figure 28 Building the Mesh

The VeriSM™ Model: Define

The VeriSM model:
Define

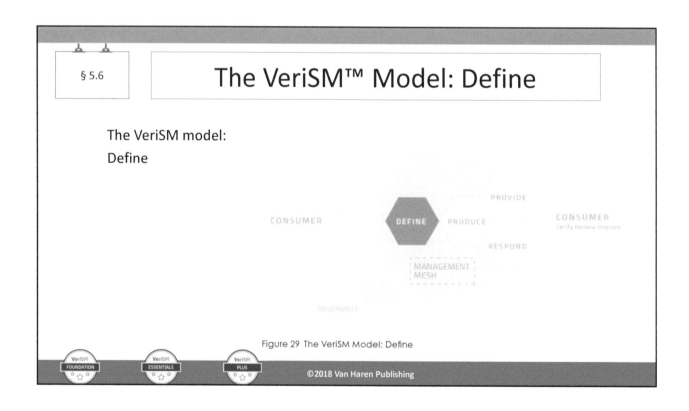

Figure 29 The VeriSM Model: Define

§ 5.6

Define Activities

Define: Activities

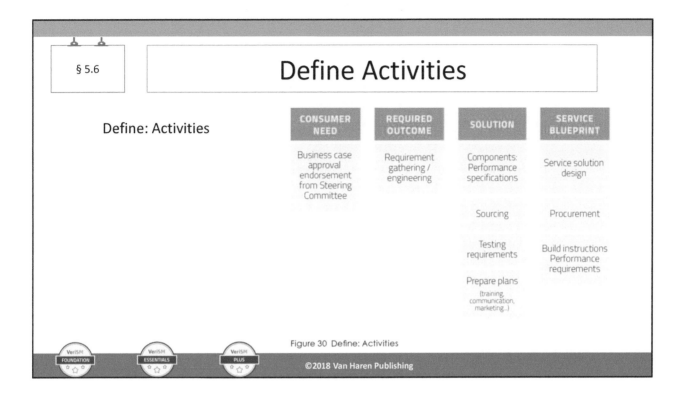

CONSUMER NEED	REQUIRED OUTCOME	SOLUTION	SERVICE BLUEPRINT
Business case approval endorsement from Steering Committee	Requirement gathering / engineering	Components: Performance specifications	Service solution design
		Sourcing	Procurement
		Testing requirements	Build instructions Performance requirements
		Prepare plans (training, communication, marketing...)	

Figure 30 Define: Activities

---

§ 5.6.1

Consumer Need

- Requirements for new products or services
  - Business case
  - Consumer request / feedback
- Accept or reject business case
  - Based on governance relating to acceptance criteria and budget capability
- Form the outline of the service blueprint
- Definition of consumer need is ongoing, requirements change over time
  - Two way communication between consumer and supplier

---

§ 5.6.2

Requirements Gathering

- Many methods for gathering requirements, both technical and non-technical
  - Interviews, workshops, town halls, meetings
- Consider both technical and non-technical requirements
  - Defines what "good" looks like from a consumer perspective
  - Information and functional requirements
  - Any changes to operational requirements
  - Organizational factors
- Design is dependent on stakeholder capabilities

©2018 Van Haren Publishing

---

§ 5.6.3

Create a Solution

- The design of the full solution includes:
  - Risk
  - People
  - Supply chain or network
  - Facilities, infrastructure and technology aspects
  - Transactions
  - Measurement and metrics
  - Knowledge capture
  - Support processes and procedures

©2018 Van Haren Publishing

---

§ 5.6.4   Create the Blueprint

- Blueprint details the design specifications including:
  - Service components, hardware, software, infrastructure, facilities and data
  - Testing and performance requirements
  - Communication plan and training requirements
  - Implementation strategy and specifications for early life support and support services
- Outlines
  - How product or service meets agreed requirements, service management principles
- Guiding document for Produce stage
  - Informs design activities, assist investigation of performance issues, improvement of all stages of the VeriSM model

---

§ 5.7   The VeriSM™ Model: Produce

The VeriSM model:
Produce

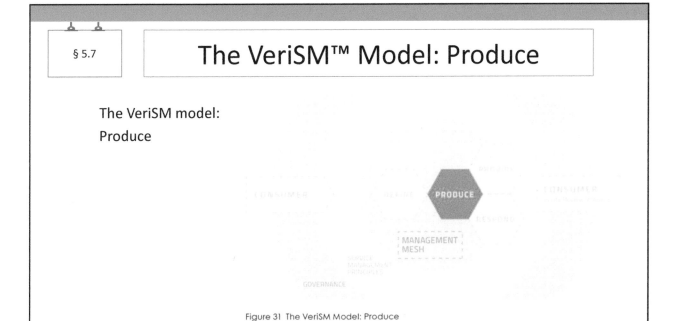

Figure 31 The VeriSM Model: Produce

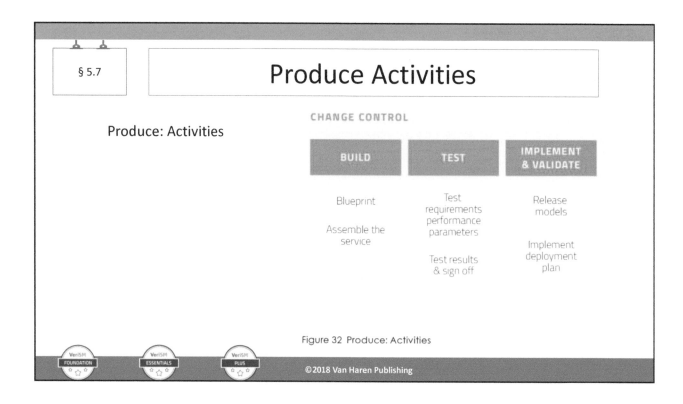

Figure 32 Produce: Activities

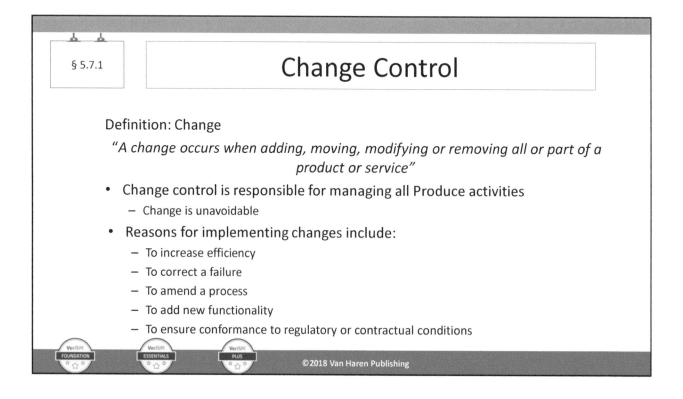

§ 5.7.1

Change Control

- All change involves risk
  - Need to be controlled and understood, minimize adverse side-effects
  - Deliver intended benefits, seen as a central process in service management
- Change management process
  - Traditional: Request and justification, review, approval or rejection, management through development and deployment, implemented and reviewed
  - Challenge to maintain sufficient control with traditional change process working in Agile, Lean and DevOps
  - Service management principles, the Management Mesh and consumer requirements drive which approach to adopt, agile or traditional
- Change activities may be automated or manual, but must be within service management principles guardrails

§ 5.7.1

Change Control Activities

- Record: change record should include what is to be changed and the expected impact on other elements
  - Initially the information will be basic, but more information will be gathered and should be verified as the process continues, to avoid incorrect approval or rejection
- Plan: change activities should be planned and scheduled according to organizational need and availability of resources
  - The plan should be communicated to all stakeholders and consumers affected
- Approve: the change should be approved
  - Appropriate approval mechanisms should be used
- Review: following the implementation the change should be reviewed
  - Are there lessons to be learned?

§ 5.7.2

Produce Activities 1

Build

- This activity uses the service blueprint to build the new product or service and supporting systems
    - Included is managing the supply chain for the procurement and delivery of the required components, items of technology or entire services
    - A lead service provider may act as a 'service integrator' to ensure all elements work together – this approach is covered in the principles of SIAM later in the course
    - Build activity includes procurement of the necessary components
        - Recoding component details for asset control and tracking
    - Readiness of the organizational capabilities
- Once everything is in place, the service is built based on the service blueprint

§ 5.7.3

Produce Activities 2

Test

- Ensure product or service operates in accordance with design plans
    - Testing levels must satisfy the organization's governance requirements for all situations
- Types of testing:
    - Functional; usability; regression; compatibility
- Testing will be driven by the organizational governance and service management principles

§ 5.7.4 — Produce Activities 3

Implement and validate

- Once testing has been declared acceptable, the new product or service will be implemented
  - According to the agreed timeframes, delivery method, requirements
  - Using the management practices identified in the Management Mesh
- Review of functionality and performance
  - Live environment may be different to test environment
- Review process to create service
  - Any improvement in time, resources, cost

©2018 Van Haren Publishing

---

§ 5.8 — The VeriSM™ Model: Provide

The VeriSM Model:

Provide

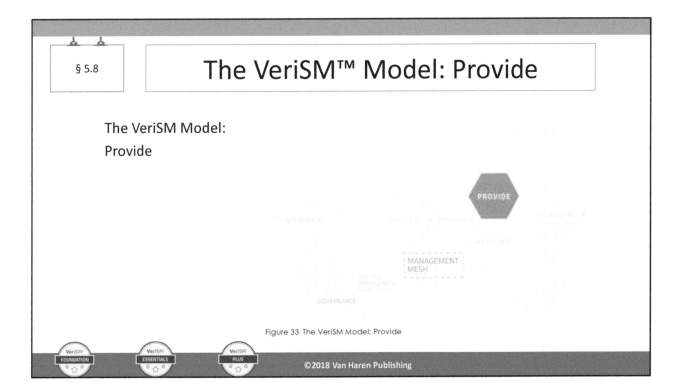

Figure 33 The VeriSM Model: Provide

©2018 Van Haren Publishing

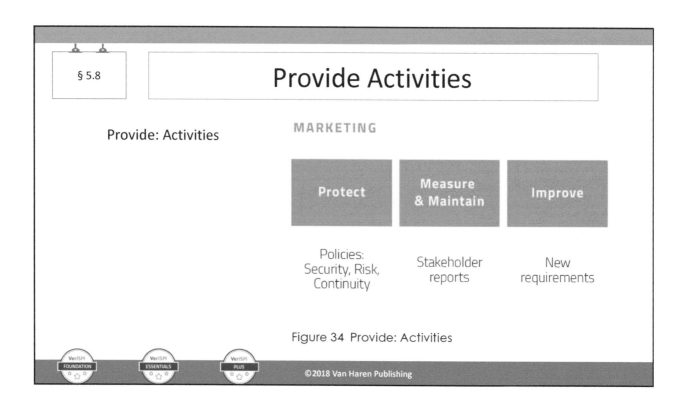

§ 5.8

Provide Activities

Provide: Activities

MARKETING

Protect

Measure & Maintain

Improve

Policies: Security, Risk, Continuity

Stakeholder reports

New requirements

Figure 34 Provide: Activities

©2018 Van Haren Publishing

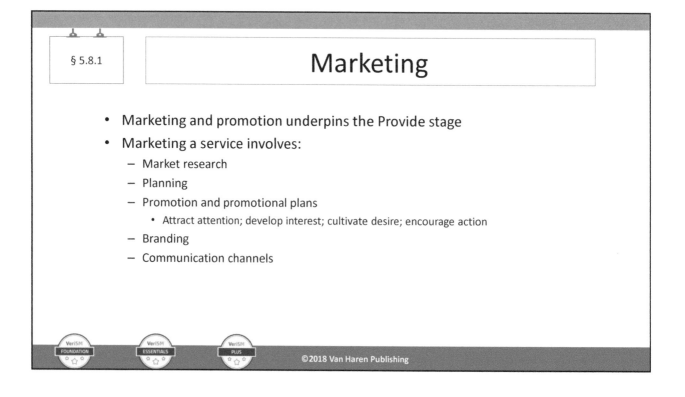

§ 5.8.1

Marketing

- Marketing and promotion underpins the Provide stage
- Marketing a service involves:
  - Market research
  - Planning
  - Promotion and promotional plans
    - Attract attention; develop interest; cultivate desire; encourage action
  - Branding
  - Communication channels

©2018 Van Haren Publishing

§ 5.8.1.3

Promotional Development

Steps in Promotional Development

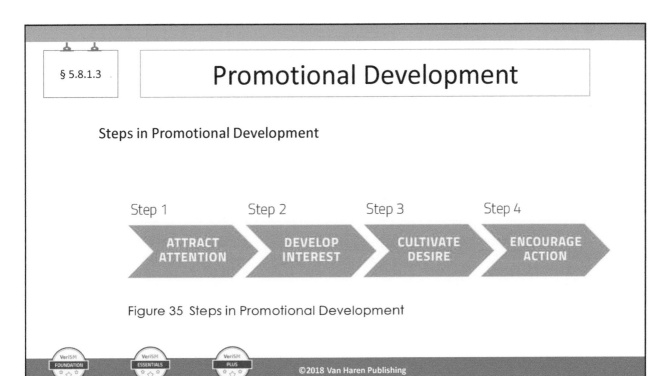

Figure 35 Steps in Promotional Development

---

§ 5.8.2

Provide Activity 1

Protect

- Security is a shared responsibility between provider and consumer
  - Providers carry out the technical activities
  - Consumers need to follow working practices relating to security
- Security policy is defined by the organization covering data, information and physical security:
  - Use of technology and disposal of technology
  - Passwords
  - Access to services, data, information and controlled areas

§ 5.8.3

Provide Activity 2

Maintain

- An on-going activity, ensuring the level of service provided consistently meets the agreed performance levels
- Data, Information and Knowledge
- Asset information
- Keep information and knowledge up to date

§ 5.8.4

Provide Activity 3

Improve

- Identification of new functionality, capability, or addressing weak areas
  - Lack of innovation may drive consumers to another provider
- Improvement opportunities
  - Identified, captured, assessed, actioned if appropriate
- Improvement areas:
  - New product or service or emerging technologies
  - Measurement results, improving delivery
  - Sourcing strategies, acquisitions, mergers, right-sizing
  - Social or environmental concerns

§ 5.9 — The VeriSM™ Model: Respond

The VeriSM model:
Respond

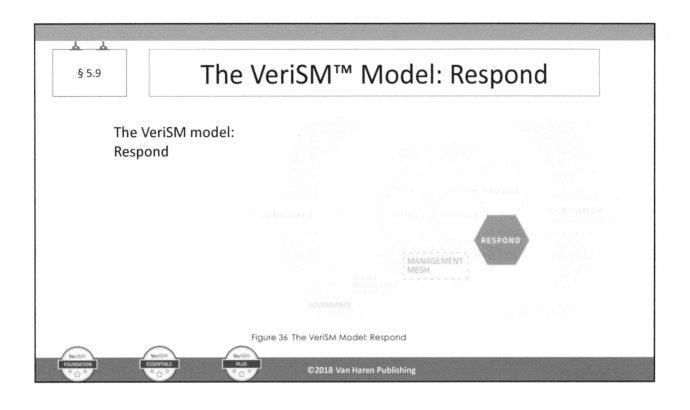

Figure 36 The VeriSM Model: Respond

§ 5.9 — Respond Activities

Respond: Activities

Figure 37 Respond: Activities

§ 5.9.1

VeriSM Responds to...

- Requests
  - Record and manage requests and failures separately
- Issues
  - Covers interactions when something is not working as expected or a consumer cannot use the service
- Source Events
  - Causes of issues, to understand why issues occurred and prevent them

©2018 Van Haren Publishing

---

§ 5.9.2

Respond Activity 1

Record
- Defines a single point of contact for all interactions
- Record all interactions, including with those who are not consumers
- High quality service is dependent on understanding interactions
- Each contact should be recorded, with a minimum set of information
- Each record should have an owner, to ensure it is managed as required
- Tools used to record and manage information need to support the organizations requirements
- Sufficient information should be held, without unnecessary capture

©2018 Van Haren Publishing

---

§ 5.9.3

Respond Activity 2

Manage

- Events may be managed directly or indirectly
  - Consumers expect multiple channels of access to support
- Support structures are adapting to new ways of interaction with consumers
  - Live support is likely to continue for most organizations
- Respond stage delivers a consistent dependable service for the consumer
- Once recorded, an issue or request will be managed through to resolution
- Communication with the consumer should be open and transparent
- Respond stage may be the only consumer interaction, needs a positive impression

©2018 Van Haren Publishing

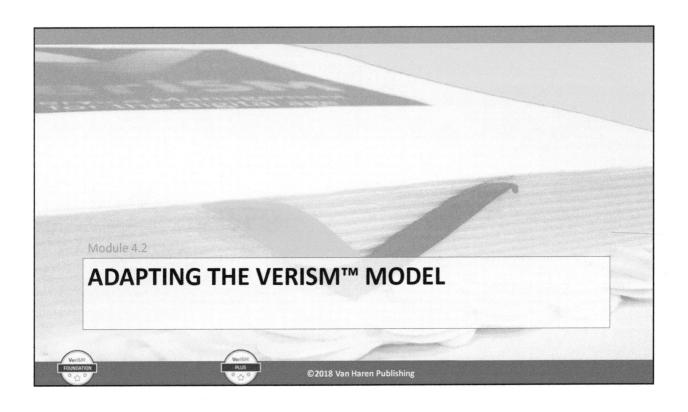

Module 4.2

ADAPTING THE VERISM™ MODEL

©2018 Van Haren Publishing

Adapting The VeriSM™ Model

§ 5.10

- Adapting the VeriSM model
  - Management practices need to be selected to suit the organizational requirements
  - No single solution or management practice will fit all situations
  - VeriSM encourages the organization to exploit the most suitable management practices for each situation
  - Combination of management practices to deliver the most value to the organization and its consumers

©2018 Van Haren Publishing

Adapting The VeriSM™ Model

§ 5.10.1

Adapting the VeriSM Model

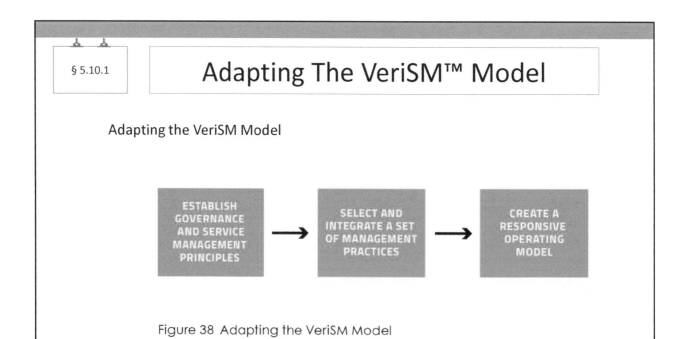

Figure 38 Adapting the VeriSM Model

©2018 Van Haren Publishing

§ 5.10 How to Integrate Management Practices

- Avoid development of silos, which can lead to a lack of cooperation and other issues
- Define the scope, responsibilities, target, measures and interfaces for each practice
- Encourage communication and collaboration across practices
  - For example Kanban boards, team briefings across disciplines
- Cross-skill training, to enable staff to become familiar with other management practices
- Use the Management Mesh to manage all management practices, resources, environments and emerging technologies
  - Flexibility is key, regular review and amendment as necessary

§ 5.10 Characteristics of Successful Operating Models

- Moving from a silo based organization to a collaborative approach
  - Challenges for senior management, staff perceptions and resistance
- Organizational change management
  - A program used to break down resistance and deliver the target operating state
- Executive sponsorship
  - Leadership from the top of the organization, through communication and championship
- Engagement
  - Staff must feel part of the change, utilize workshops, company meetings, feedback sessions, focus groups to achieve buy-in
  - Staff actively involved will be more enthusiastic and cooperative

§ 5.10

Characteristics of Successful Operating Models

- Enablement
  - IT and other systems must support the new operating model
  - Organizational structure should facilitate the new operating model
  - Incentives can reward new behaviors, such as team collaboration
- Measurement
  - Inertia is one of the biggest challenges to organizational change
  - Reporting that shows improvement and progress towards a goal will motivate staff
  - Measurement of success is critical to the communication of the new operating model
  - Reporting must identify, quantify and publish the results of success
  - Two distinct areas for measurement, the consumer and the service provider

  ©2018 Van Haren Publishing

---

§ 5.10.6

Measuring the Operating Model

Services Deliver Results

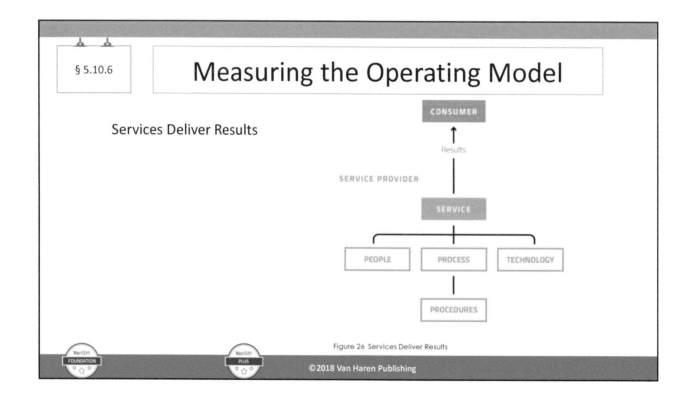

Figure 26 Services Deliver Results

©2018 Van Haren Publishing

§ 5.10.6

Measuring Consumer and Service Provider

- Consumer:
  - Value is based on whether the service delivers or enables the required outcomes
  - A service is valuable if the perceived service benefit exceeds the cost of receiving it
- Service provider:
  - Service provider needs to understand and measure from the consumer's perspective
  - Measurements are used to verify that the value of the service justifies the cost and effort to deliver it
  - Needs to understand how well the underpinning service elements, technology or applications are working

---

§ 5.10.6

Value Measurement

- Value perception in service measurement considers
  - Consumer - how valuable does the consumer perceive the service to be?
  - Organization - does the service meet the mission, vision and goals?
  - Provider – how does the value compare with the cost of provision?
  - Compliance – are there any applicable laws, regulations and contractual commitments
- Service measurements focus on the outcome or results
- Perspective of all stakeholders should be covered
- Measures must be:
  - Cost-effective; balanced; adaptable; up-to-date

---

§ 5.10.6.1

Quality

Definition: Quality

'a measure of excellence or freedom from defects, variations and deficiencies'

- A provider should define a stated level of quality, influenced by
  - Service provider's reputation, brand, industry standards, laws and regulations
- Perceived value depends on the perceived quality
- Consumer wants the best quality service for the price they can pay
  - Governed by the value of the outcome the service supports
  - Delivered within time and price constraints
- Provider wants to deliver service to consumers that is cost justifiable on the return achieved

©2018 Van Haren Publishing

---

§ 5.10.6.2

Service Measurement Benefits

- Enables fact-based decision making; provides a benchmark for later comparison
- Identifies potential areas for improvement; confirms the performance and value of a service;
- Facilitates trend analysis; shares information and knowledge about a service;
- Supports an understanding of the demand for a service;
- Brings transparency into the delivery of a service;
- Supports an understanding of the cost of service provisioning (from the service provider perspective);
- Supports an understanding of the cost of service consumption (from the consumer perspective)

©2018 Van Haren Publishing

---

§ 5.10.6.3

Reporting

- Reporting influences the perception of the value of a service
- Service measurement requires reporting to be delivered to the consumer
  - Enables consumer to assess the value of the services provided
  - Service provider needs reporting to enable management of the service
- Reporting must be:
  - Relevant
  - Timely
  - Appropriate for the audience
    - Needs of consumers, service providers and senior managers are all different

---

§ 5.10.7

Report Design

- Report design determines what and how to report service measures
  - Ensure the report is needed before producing
- Reporting must be timely to be useful
- A key factor in determining the frequency, time frame and detail is understanding how the report will be used
- A reporting function must be able to address all of these requirements

---

Module 4

Quiz questions

- Which of these are elements of the VeriSM model?
1. Define
2. Produce
3. Provide
4. Respond

a) 1, 2 & 3
b) 1, 2 & 4
c) 2, 3 & 4
d) All of the above

Module 4

Quiz questions

- Which of these are elements of the VeriSM model?
1. Define
2. Produce
3. Provide
4. Respond

a) 1, 2 & 3
b) 1, 2 & 4
c) 2, 3 & 4
d) All of the above

Module 4

Quiz questions

- What does this describe?

"The combination of resources, environment, emerging technologies and management practices"

a) Governance
b) Activities
c) Management Mesh
d) Service management principles

Module 4

Quiz questions

- What does this describe?

"The combination of resources, environment, emerging technologies and management practices"

a) Governance
b) Activities
c) Management Mesh
d) Service management principles

Quiz questions

- VeriSM re-defines the term service provider. Which of these reflects the definition of a service provider in VeriSM?

a) The service integrator is the sole service provider
b) Consumers are the service providers of their own services
c) The entire organization is a service provider
d) The IT department is the sole service provider

Quiz questions

- VeriSM re-defines the term service provider. Which of these reflects the definition of a service provider in VeriSM?

a) The service integrator is the sole service provider
b) Consumers are the service providers of their own services
c) The entire organization is a service provider
d) The IT department is the sole service provider

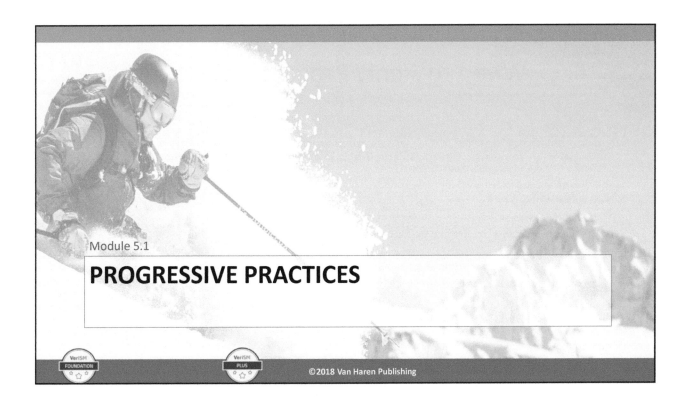

Progressive Practices

- Developed in response to emerging technologies, digital transformation and increased expectations
- Common success factors for progressive practices include:
  - Maintaining organizational commitment to new roles, disciplines and practices
  - A change, or at least a review, of the organizational structure
  - Supporting tools and automation are not enough on their own to create change
  - Trust and collaboration are key between capabilities
  - Not all activities will be a success, but failure is not wrong, it is a learning opportunity
  - New management practices are not a 'magic bullet' to fix everything

---

Complete table can be found in Appendix I of this courseware

When to Apply Progressive Practices

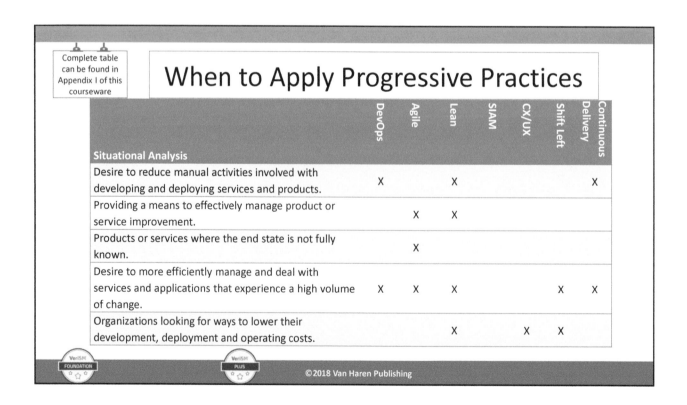

Situational Analysis	DevOps	Agile	Lean	SIAM	CX/UX	Shift Left	Continuous Delivery
Desire to reduce manual activities involved with developing and deploying services and products.	X		X				X
Providing a means to effectively manage product or service improvement.		X	X				
Products or services where the end state is not fully known.		X					
Desire to more efficiently manage and deal with services and applications that experience a high volume of change.	X	X	X			X	X
Organizations looking for ways to lower their development, deployment and operating costs.			X		X	X	

§ 6.3

Agile

- Agile Definition:
    - *"The ability to think quickly, solve problems, have new ideas and also to move quickly, be coordinated"*
- Not a single framework or standard
- Has guiding principles and values
- Agile mindset
- An Agile organization
    - Meets unexpected challenges and opportunities rapidly
    - Fast moving, flexible

  ©2018 Van Haren Publishing

---

§ 6.3

Agile

- Agile developed to address production and development working together
    - Close collaboration between programmers and other capabilities
- Deals with issues in development
    - Cost, predictability, scope creep
- Re-organizes activities to be leaner, more business focused
- Ensures delivery is what is wanted
    - Ongoing communication
    - Understanding requirements
    - Value delivered

  ©2018 Van Haren Publishing

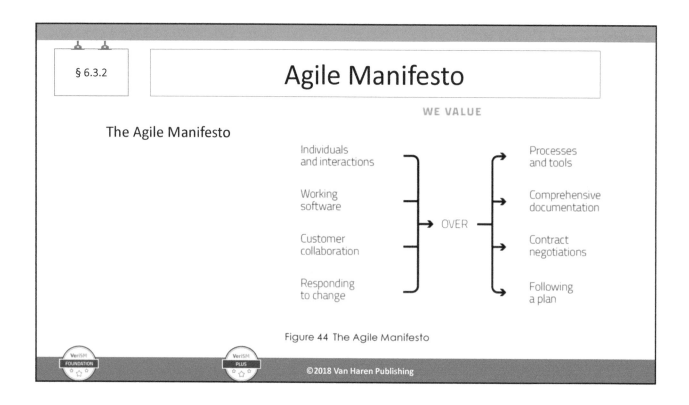

§ 6.3.2

Agile Manifesto

The Agile Manifesto

Figure 44 The Agile Manifesto

©2018 Van Haren Publishing

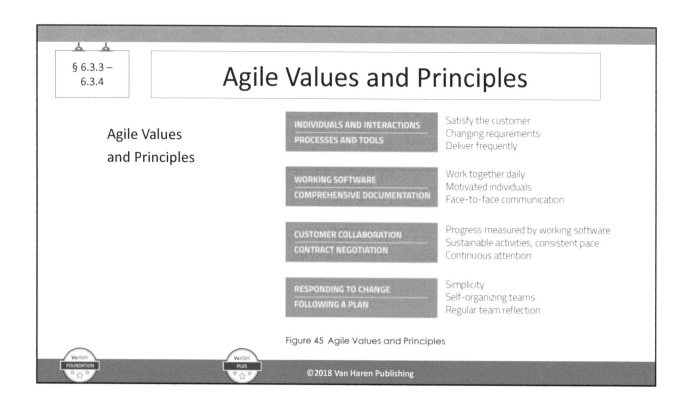

§ 6.3.3 –
6.3.4

Agile Values and Principles

Agile Values
and Principles

Figure 45 Agile Values and Principles

©2018 Van Haren Publishing

§ 6.3.1

Agile – Key Concepts

- Sprint
  - 'Time boxed iteration of work during which an increment of product functionality is developed and implemented'
  - Sprints are typically two to four weeks long, can be as short as one week
- Product backlog
  - Prioritized list of all requirements for a system, documented as backlog items
  - Product owner is responsible for prioritizing the items
  - Requirements
    - 'user stories' from the user perspective describes the 'who', 'what' and 'why'
  - Backlog items are moved into a sprint

§ 6.3.5

Agile Mindset

- Agile principles develop the agile, or growth, mindset which changes the culture of an organization

Fixed Mindset	Agile Growth Mindset
Avoiding failure	Failing fast
Avoid challenges	Embrace challenges
Resistance to change or improvement	Continual improvement
Plan in great detail	Evolving the plan based on continual feedback

Agile Benefits

- Faster delivery
- Improved stakeholder management
- Predictable costs and schedule
- Focus on value
- Adaptability
- Improved quality

©2018 Van Haren Publishing

When to Apply Agile

- Agile is appropriate for:
  - Organizations who need to show initial results quickly, or to test and receive feedback
  - Clarification of requirements, when there are concerns or requirements not understood
  - An organization needs to release new features to create revenue
  - When speed to market is required for a competitive advantage
- Agile is less appropriate for:
  - When a development scope has been fixed in a contract
  - Development teams that are very large, and geographically spread
  - Where communication is difficult within an organization, as Agile relies on the sprint
  - A project has a rigid structure

©2018 Van Haren Publishing

VeriSM™ – Foundation Courseware

©2018 Van Haren Publishing

§ 6.4

DevOps

- Developed from the IT community to improve relationships between development and operations teams
  - Cultural aspects of DevOps address the potential development and operations conflicts
  - Cross functional teams own a product or service throughout all project stages
  - Collaboration approach allows for review and improvement across the project
  - Solutions built, deployed and operable with minimal delays
- DevOps replaces the traditional handover between development and quality assurances and operational teams
- Operational focus remains on supporting new solutions
- DevOps promotes and supports continuous testing and delivery, automation, Agile and Lean

©2018 Van Haren Publishing

---

§ 6.4.2

DevOps Values

- DevOps values 'CALMS':
  - Culture
    - Communication, collaboration and teamwork in operating behaviors
  - Automation
    - Removal of manual steps reduces errors, increases operating speeds, consistent standards
  - Lean
    - Flow and pull can create more value for consumers with fewer resources
  - Measurement
    - Essential to demonstrate value, with regular review and actions to address issues
  - Sharing
    - Communication, collaboration supporting continual improvement

©2018 Van Haren Publishing

VeriSM™ – Foundation Courseware

©2018 Van Haren Publishing

§ 6.4.1

DevOps in the VeriSM Model

The VeriSM model:

DevOps

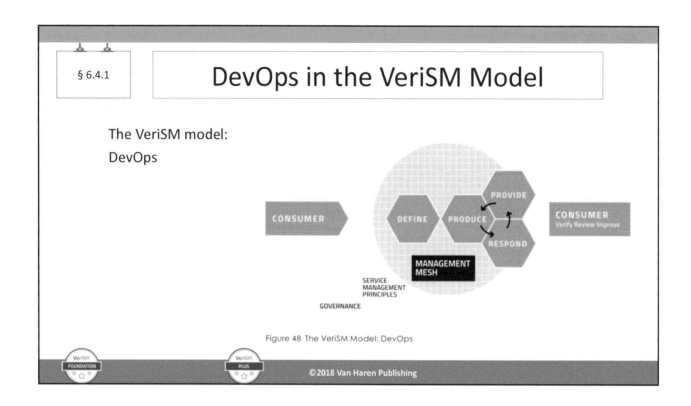

Figure 48 The VeriSM Model: DevOps

---

§ 6.4.3

The Three Ways of DevOps

Core philosophies of DevOps:

- First way: flow and thinking
  - Understand the flow left to right, remove bottlenecks
- Second way: feedback
  - Shorter feedback loops for continuous improvement
- Third way: continuous experimentation and learning
  - Fail fast and move on, without fear

VeriSM™ – Foundation Courseware

§ 6.4.4

DevOps Supporting Practices

- Continuous testing
  - Automated test facilities which respond automatically to a change
- Continuous delivery
  - Automated deployment in response to change
- Automation for velocity
  - Automation to increase speed in development across the application lifecycle management process
- Infrastructure as code
  - Also known as Declarative Configuration Management, infrastructure build and provisioning can be automated

  ©2018 Van Haren Publishing

---

§ 6.4.5 –
6.4.5

When to Apply DevOps

- DevOps will be appropriate for:
  - Organizations requiring quick delivery of business value or removal of defects in software deployments
  - Breakdown of silos in development and operations, or reducing labor in the development cycle
  - Rapid changes immediately after deployment
- DevOps will not be appropriate for:
  - Organizations with little or no management support for collaborative approaches
  - Organizations that do not recognize the value of CALMS

  ©2018 Van Haren Publishing

VeriSM™ – Foundation Courseware

©2018 Van Haren Publishing

§ 6.5

Service Integration and Management (SIAM)

- Set of management practices and principles
  - Manage, integrate, govern and coordinate service delivery from multiple suppliers
- Service integrator
  - Single impartial point of contact for the management of services
  - Maximize value for money from suppliers
- Service broker
  - Managing service provision from multiple service providers

---

§ 6.5.1

SIAM Ecosystem

A SIAM ecosystem

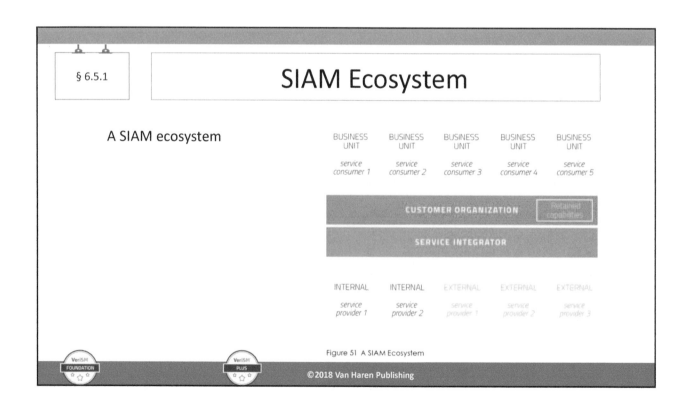

Figure 51 A SIAM Ecosystem

SIAM Key Concepts

§ 6.5.2 – 6.5.5

- Service broker
  - Service broker provides access for its clients to a range of products and services via a single point of contact
  - Sourcing mechanism drawing together services or component from many providers and delivering to meet a customer requirement via a single point of contact
  - More complexity in service provision, more challenges to overcome
- SIAM has developed from outsourcing
  - Allowing organizations to focus on their core business
  - Benefits include lower costs, savings in time, effort, manpower, operating and training costs, capital expenditure, shared business risks, even permanent headcount reduction
- Disadvantages include
  - Management of legacy contracts, loss of internal knowledge, greater threats to security

  ©2018 Van Haren Publishing

When to Apply SIAM

§ 6.5.6 – 6.5.7

- SIAM is appropriate for:
  - Organizations that will derive real benefits from sourcing externally
  - Optimizing an approach to supplier management for better service delivery
  - Supplier governance with multiple suppliers, or those increasing supplier engagement
  - Engagement with technologies outside of the organizational scope
- SIAM is less appropriate for:
  - Organizations where there is a reliance on a limited number of suppliers
  - A product or service that is unique and hard to source from elsewhere
  - A situation where the organization is unable to make decisions across multiple business units

  ©2018 Van Haren Publishing

§ 6.5.9 — SIAM and Service Management

- SIAM is underpinned by many service management practices
- For SIAM to be successful:
  - An organization needs to be clear on what will be outsourced and what will be retained
  - Commissioning organization needs to retain overall control
    - Have the skills necessary to negotiate and manage contracts
    - Have the skills necessary to measure and report on suppliers
  - All parties need to understand the complexity of the arrangement
  - The SIAM model needs to be commercially beneficial to all parties
  - Service providers must be able to work collaboratively with potential competitors
  - All organizations in the ecosystem should have a good cultural fit

  ©2018 Van Haren Publishing

§ 6.6 — Lean

- The goal of Lean is to maximize consumer value, whilst minimizing waste
  - A perfect Lean solution would be to provide value to a consumer with zero waste
- Lean practices and concepts apply across the whole VeriSM model
- Lean is an ongoing way of thinking and operating, requiring transformation
- Three fundamental issues to consider for a Lean transformation:
  - Purpose: what obstacles to achieving organizational objectives will be removed by the actions
  - Process: how will waste be eradicated in the organizational value streams
  - People: how will the organization ensure accountability, ownership and continual improvement for each critical value stream and process

  ©2018 Van Haren Publishing

Lean Principles

Lean Principles

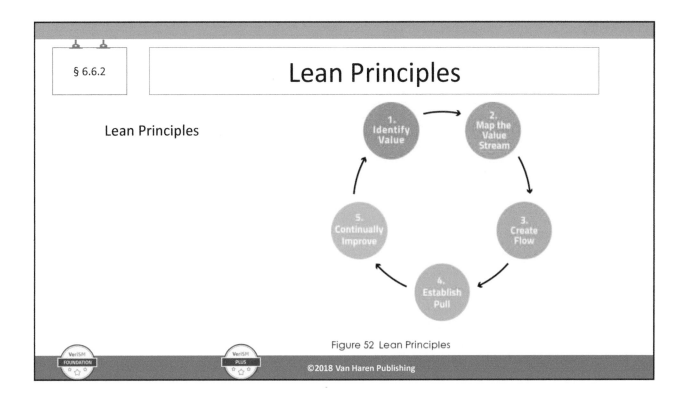

Figure 52 Lean Principles

©2018 Van Haren Publishing

Lean Key Concepts

- Flow
  - How products and services move through a process
  - Good flow is work moving steadily and predictably
  - Bad flow has bottlenecks, and potentially no clear process design
- Pull
  - Making sure there is no waste between work steps
  - Batching work is considered to be inefficient, as waiting for batches causes delays
  - Errors will put the whole batch at risk
  - Pull eliminates this waste as processes operate with 'single piece flow'

©2018 Van Haren Publishing

VeriSM™ – Foundation Courseware

©2018 Van Haren Publishing

§ 6.6.4

Lean Key Concepts

- Waste
  - Time spent on activities that add no value to the process, or produce defects
- Lean recognizes two general types of waste:
  - Necessary waste – does not appear to deliver value, but is required to happen,
  - Unnecessary waste – does not add value, a defect or waiting time
- Specific waste types include:
  - Cascading waste, where one element of a process causes delays further down the process flow
  - Inventory; waiting; defects

©2018 Van Haren Publishing

---

§ 6.6.5

Lean Key Concepts

- Takt time
  - Determined by the rate of demand from the customer
  - Each step should have the same takt time creating a balanced flow of work
- Cycle time
  - The total time needed to receive a product or service
  - Defined by service provider and customer
  - Includes process time, when work takes place, and delay time, waiting for the next action

©2018 Van Haren Publishing

VeriSM™ – Foundation Courseware

©2018 Van Haren Publishing

§ 6.6.6

Value Stream Mapping

- Value stream mapping:
  - Select and scope the process to be mapped
  - Define what the value is from the customer's viewpoint
  - Collect data and observe the actual work in 'Gemba'
  - Map the current state of the value stream
  - Identify waste in the current value stream
  - Analyze the data for trends, relations and root causes
  - Map the future process state
  - Develop a transition plan to move to this future state

  ©2018 Van Haren Publishing

§ 6.6.7 – 6.6.8

When to Apply Lean

- Lean is appropriate for:
  - An organization looking for ways to improve processes that are ineffective
  - Organizations looking to lower their operating costs, or continuously improve services or production
  - Organizations needing to meet service targets and consumer expectations, stop firefighting
- Lean is not appropriate for:
  - Situations when the costs of start-up are greater than the potential gains
  - Non-service or product situations, for example reducing headcount
  - Innovation, as this requires the generation of failure to prove a concept
  - Unpredictable demand, or large scale issues in a short time frame

  ©2018 Van Haren Publishing

Lean and Service Management

- Lean and Service Management
  - Processes assessed for waste
  - Create a value stream map, identify delays or inefficiencies, fix the biggest problem
  - Continue to assess the process to eliminate waste
- Lean requires ongoing management
  - Using tools and techniques such as grouping services into families, for similar process flows, then applying improvement across multiple services
  - Tasks that clarify information or remove defects should be at the start of the process, known as front loading
  - Remove bottlenecks, but if one is removed, often another will appear
  - Lean recommends dispatchers handle the flow of work through a process to improve flow

©2018 Van Haren Publishing

Shift Left

How Shift Left Works

Apply Shift Left principles to:
- Support
- Testing
- Deployment

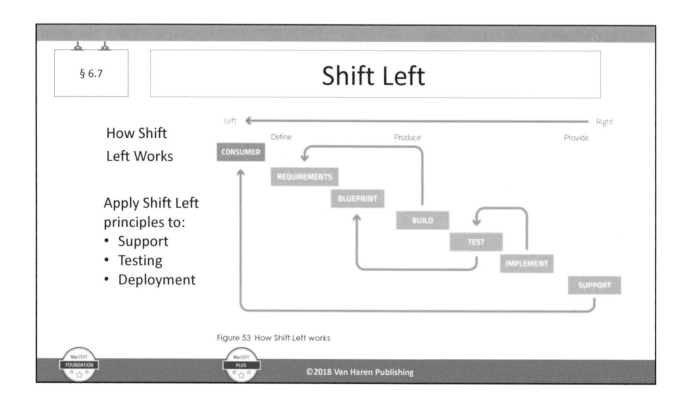

Figure 53 How Shift Left works

©2018 Van Haren Publishing

---

§ 6.7.1

Necessary Capabilities for Shift Left

- Knowledge management
  - Requires shared knowledge both within and external to the organization
  - Automated systems need information to interrogate to provide answers
- Self service
  - Allows consumers to access and receive a service directly
  - Potentially delivering a wide range of services, through multiple media
  - Can be perceived as 'hiding' from the consumer unless properly introduced
- Automation
  - Benefits include increased speed of task completion, cost reductions, reduced human error, increased capability, consistency and adaptability

---

§ 6.7.3 – 6.7.4

When to Apply Shift Left

- Shift Left is appropriate for:
  - Organizations needing to make improvements faster or earlier in the development cycle
  - Improvement of collaboration between development, testing and operations teams
  - Assisting with the management of testing and quality assurance bottlenecks
  - Potentially lowering costs for fixing defects
- Shift Left is not appropriate for:
  - An organization with little or no collaboration or investment in the development, testing and operations teams
  - Organizations that are strongly resistant to change, or where cost savings are the sole interest, or lack a knowledge management approach

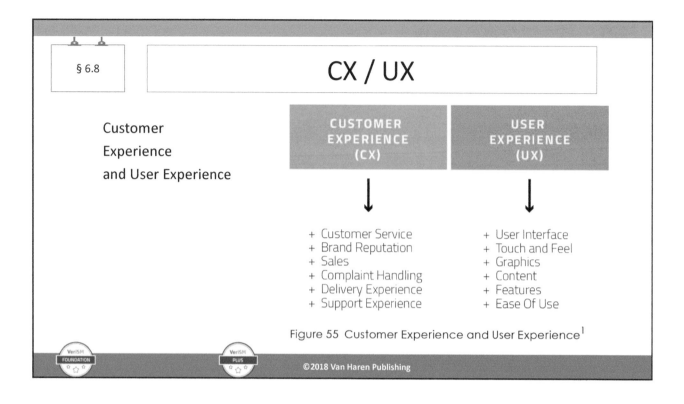

§ 6.8

CX / UX

Customer
Experience
and User Experience

CUSTOMER EXPERIENCE (CX)	USER EXPERIENCE (UX)
+ Customer Service	+ User Interface
+ Brand Reputation	+ Touch and Feel
+ Sales	+ Graphics
+ Complaint Handling	+ Content
+ Delivery Experience	+ Features
+ Support Experience	+ Ease Of Use

Figure 55 Customer Experience and User Experience[1]

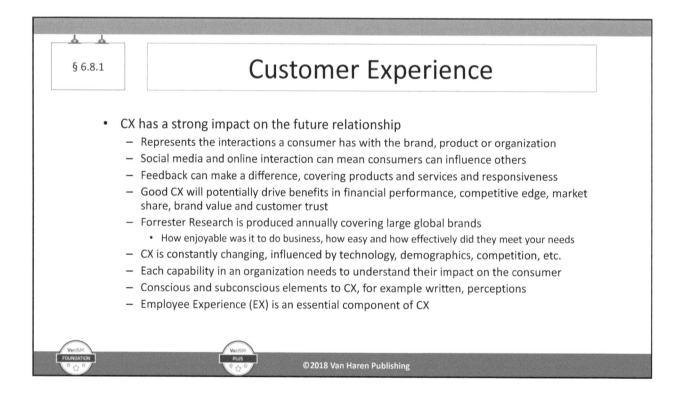

§ 6.8.1

Customer Experience

- CX has a strong impact on the future relationship
  - Represents the interactions a consumer has with the brand, product or organization
  - Social media and online interaction can mean consumers can influence others
  - Feedback can make a difference, covering products and services and responsiveness
  - Good CX will potentially drive benefits in financial performance, competitive edge, market share, brand value and customer trust
  - Forrester Research is produced annually covering large global brands
    - How enjoyable was it to do business, how easy and how effectively did they meet your needs
  - CX is constantly changing, influenced by technology, demographics, competition, etc.
  - Each capability in an organization needs to understand their impact on the consumer
  - Conscious and subconscious elements to CX, for example written, perceptions
  - Employee Experience (EX) is an essential component of CX

§ 6.8.3 | User Experience

- UX is critical for any digital product or service
  - UX explores the feelings of the user, not the interaction of the user interface, which is a technical relationship between human / computer
  - UX needs to be a rich engagement with simple and easy to use interactions, if it does not function as expected, consumers will not use it
  - DX can meet or exceed consumer expectations, dependent on how well it integrates into the product or service

---

§ 6.8.5 | Net Promoter Score

Net Promoter Score

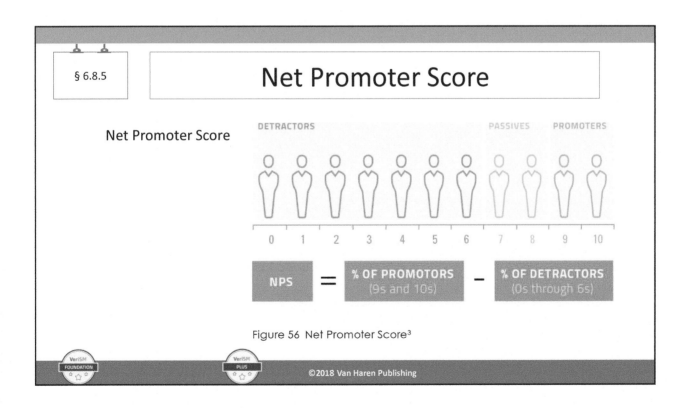

Figure 56 Net Promoter Score[3]

VeriSM™ – Foundation Courseware

§ 6.8.6

CX / UX

- Organizations need to design for both user and customer experience
  - Design should enhance and provide for each set of needs
- CX covers every touchpoint and interaction with the consumer
- UX is a specific component concerned with the usability of the product or service
- Balance is required
- Good CX can overcome poor UX
  - If there is a usability issue, the way it is handled can leave a consumer with a good overall experience

©2018 Van Haren Publishing

---

§ 6.8.7 – 6.8.8

When to Apply CX / UX

- CX / UX is appropriate for:
  - Organizations who want to differentiate their brand, product or service, to capture or retain market share
  - Organizations who wish to match their development strategy to consumer needs
  - Organizations that are concerned with improving consumer satisfaction, or wish to be seen as innovative
- CX / UX is not appropriate for:
  - Organizations whose products or services are not based on competition, or they have a reputation and NPS value that exceeds any gain from investment
  - Organizations who have no skills in the principles of CX / UX as this will contribute to additional costs

©2018 Van Haren Publishing

---

§ 6.9

Continuous Delivery

- Continuous Delivery
  - Management practice, not a technical solution
  - Requires significant management planning and support, not just technology
  - Continuous integration of software completed by development, and testing
  - Output from testing is tried in production like environments
  - Framework for deployment to happen quickly, supporting Agile and DevOps
- Not the same as continuous deployment
  - Continuous deployment enable frequent deployment
  - Continuous delivery is delivering to a pre-production environment and performing testing

©2018 Van Haren Publishing

§ 6.9.1

Continuous Delivery

- Automated tests in production-like environments
- Assure software operates as designed and is always in a deployable state
- Removes the need for a testing and integration phase at the end of the project
- If testing and integration phases are skipped at the end of a project it can lead to technical debt, and errors will be more expensive to fix

Definition: Technical debt

"Technical debt is a term in software development that reflects the extra development work that arises when code which is easy to implement in the short run is used instead of applying the best overall solution."

©2018 Van Haren Publishing

VeriSM™ – Foundation Courseware

§ 6.9.1 — Continuous Delivery Key Concepts

- Continuous integration
  - Applicable to waterfall as well as continuous delivery, it is a practice where developers integrate code into a shared repository daily – this is a 'commit'
- Continuous deployment
  - Enables every change that passes automated tests to be automatically deployed to production
- Continuous testing
  - A test facility is constantly operational, using automation to execute test and monitor results

§ 6.9.2 – 6.9.3 — When to Apply Continuous Delivery

- Continuous delivery is appropriate for:
  - Organizations that are already using Agile, Lean, DevOps or Shift Left practices, who want to maximize the benefits they are receiving from these practices
  - Organizations that want to minimize the traditional delays of testing, by reducing the risks of testing and fixing errors before they become expensive
  - Developers who are geographically scattered, or have many teams, by ensuring there is consistent testing across all teams
- Continuous delivery is not appropriate for:
  - Organizations who do not have adequate toolsets to deliver automated testing
  - Organizations where the rate of change is reducing, making this approach expensive
  - Organizations who do not have sufficient funding, or scale of operation, to warrant this approach

Module 5

Quiz questions

- Common success factors for progressive practices include which of these concepts?
1. Senior management commitment
2. Review of the organizational structure
3. Trust and collaboration between capabilities

a) 1 and 2 only
b) 1, 2 & 3
c) 1 and 3 only
d) 2 and 3 only

Module 5

Quiz questions

- Common success factors for progressive practices include which of these concepts?
1. Senior management commitment
2. Review of the organizational structure
3. Trust and collaboration between capabilities

a) 1 and 2 only
b) 1, 2 & 3
c) 1 and 3 only
d) 2 and 3 only

Module 5

Quiz questions

- Which progressive practice is described as having four values, supported by twelve principles, embracing rapid change cycles?

a) Agile
b) DevOps
c) ITIL
d) Lean

©2018 Van Haren Publishing

Module 5

Quiz questions

- Which progressive practice is described as having four values, supported by twelve principles, embracing rapid change cycles?

a) Agile
b) DevOps
c) ITIL
d) Lean

©2018 Van Haren Publishing

VeriSM™ – Foundation Courseware

©2018 Van Haren Publishing

Module 5

Quiz questions

- Which progressive practice has a service integrator as a key element of its structure?

a) ITIL
b) Agile
c) DevOps
d) SIAM

Module 5

Quiz questions

- Which progressive practice has a service integrator as a key element of its structure?

a) ITIL
b) Agile
c) DevOps
d) SIAM

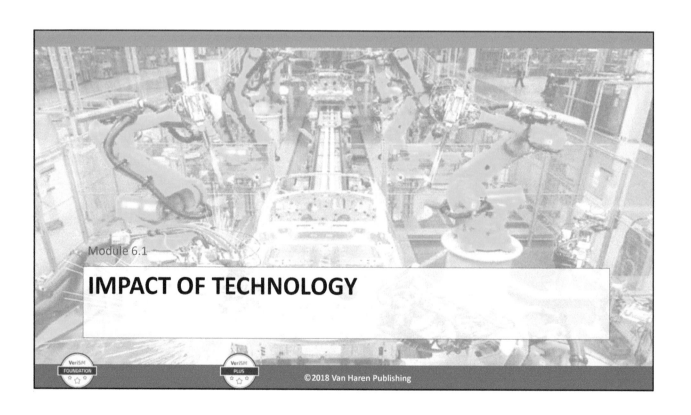

§ 7.1

Impact of Technology

- Innovative technologies
  - Part of the Management Mesh, along with environment, resources, and management practices
  - Organizations need to assess new technologies, to decide if they will be useful when developing a new product or service
- Service management implications:
  - There is a risk of the technology dictating the solution, rather than the consumer requirement
  - Unwanted new functionality may be a waste of time and resources
  - Engagement of the consumers from the start of the development, avoiding assumptions
  - New technology is used to meet a requirement, not just because its new

  ©2018 Van Haren Publishing

§ 7.1

Technology and VeriSM

- Organizations adopting the VeriSM model need to understand emerging technologies and keep the knowledge up to date
  - Ensure the service management principles and the Management Mesh accurately reflect technical capabilities
- Staff need to:
  - Ensure the service provider staff have the correct specialist or generalist knowledge
  - Understand the knowledge requirements for staff in business capability areas
  - Understand the sourcing model and where responsibilities rest
  - Assess the maturity level of the organization and readiness to adopt emergent technologies

  ©2018 Van Haren Publishing

Cloud Computing

§ 7.2

- Cloud computing
  - Hosting services managed by an external cloud service provider (CSP). Internet based provision of on-demand computing resources - servers, storage, applications, networks
  - Cloud exploits new technologies with virtualization and automation of processes
    - Cost-effective for suppliers providing services to multiple consumers
- Cloud benefits include:
  - Minimizes the need for accurate forecasting and sizing, providing a flexible payment structure where the consumer pays for usage
  - Cloud services can flex to suit changing requirements, where internal sourcing may risk incorrect predictions and provision
  - Ownership and management of the infrastructure is with the cloud provider

  ©2018 Van Haren Publishing

Cloud Computing Benefits

§ 7.2.1

- Cloud benefits include:
  - Costs can be directly attributed to usage and demand, highlighting waste
  - Economies of scale
  - Flexible capacity
  - Cloud services can be accessed from anywhere
  - Speed of response, as resources are provisioned from a pool
- Cloud computing encourages automation
  - Automation increases the requirement for good service management
    - Automation of a poor process is ineffective and inefficient

  ©2018 Van Haren Publishing

---

§ 7.3   Virtualization

Virtualization
Example

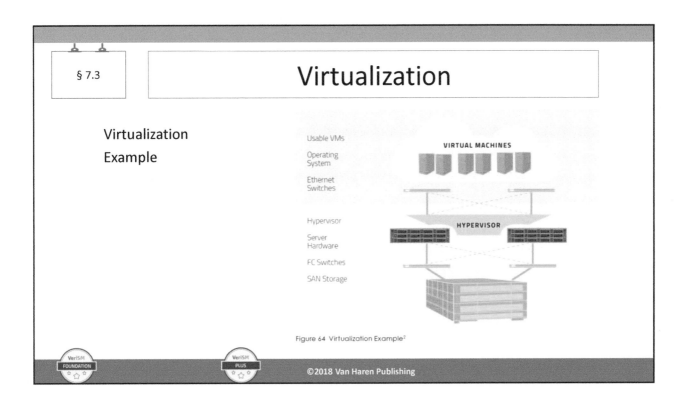

Figure 64 Virtualization Example[2]

---

§ 7.3.1   Virtualization Benefits

- Benefits of virtualization:
  - Maximizing the use of physical infrastructure components
  - A virtualized server can be restored electronically very quickly should a failure occur, reducing downtime
  - Components can be provisioned in minutes
  - Components may be moved between physical platforms to balance demand
  - Economies of scale can be achieved in licensing, warranty and support costs
  - Space requirements, power usage and environmental impact are reduced
- Virtualization enables components to be configured, restored and maintained without interruption to live service

---

VeriSM™ – Foundation Courseware

§ 7.4   Automation

- Automation has increased with evolution of IT technologies
- Automation positives include:
  - Automated codes and scripts replace human interaction and risk of human error
  - Reducing staff numbers
  - Carrying out transactions that require both speed and accuracy
  - Tasks which may otherwise be prone to errors
  - Removal of workflow bottlenecks, improved communication flows
  - Monitoring of infrastructure or tasks and the notification of events reported
  - Recovery from failures
  - Standard operating procedures

§ 7.4.1   Automation Benefits

- Benefits of automation include:
  - Speed –code and scripts are faster than people
  - Accuracy – automated tasks are consistent, reducing the chance of errors
  - Enforcement – automated tasks ensure that the required actions are carried out, and policies enforced
  - Experience – automation may improve the customer experience, leading to consumer satisfaction and repeat sales
  - Scalable – automated tasks are easier to scale to meet demand and growth
  - Cost efficiency – automation of manual activities reduces the cost of operation
- Only tasks and processes that are clearly understood, optimized and will add value should be automated

§ 7.5

Big Data

- Big data is a concept which brings business data together
  - Opportunity to mine, correlate, analyze and present insights that separate data stores cannot provide
  - Implementing a 'big data' strategy provides access to a single source for all data assets across the organization
- Organizations may struggle to put a big data strategy into practice
  - Quantity of data and multiple data formats and locations
  - Traditional technologies and databases, with limited access
- Innovative technologies support big data strategies
  - Technology can handle structured and unstructured data, observe and track data , use Machine Learning for analysis

©2018 Van Haren Publishing

§ 7.5

Big Data and Service Management

- Big data architectures include:
  - Data sources; Data platforms; Data analysis; Data visualization
- Big data and Service Management
  - Capacity management; manipulating large amounts of data requires capacity, provided in-house, or via cloud services
  - Information security; data needs to be secure
  - Knowledge management; big data approach enables information to be extracted from combined data sources
  - Financial management; analysis of data may highlight potential cost savings

©2018 Van Haren Publishing

VeriSM™ – Foundation Courseware

©2018 Van Haren Publishing

§ 7.6   Internet of Things

- Internet of Things (IoT)
  - Internet access used to be via PC or servers, then phone and tablet devices
  - Internet access is now available through many different devices, for example wearable technology, domestic appliances
- Key requirements for systems and Service Management use of IoT data:
  - Collection of data from the managed device / appliance
  - Secure connectivity
  - Monitoring of devices and data transmission, including reporting and response to alerts
  - Control mechanisms for data management

§ 7.6.1   Internet of Things Benefits

- Internet of Things benefits include:
  - Better tracking of consumer behavior to support real-time marketing
  - Process optimization
  - Automated product and service feedback
  - Better data on product and service use
  - New channels and new sales processes
  - Linking consumers more closely to the service provider

§ 7.7 Mobile Computing

- Mobile computing technologies
  - Access to IT services available from anywhere, made possible by advances in technology
- Examples of mobile computing technologies used to transmit data, voice and video include:
  - Portable computing, mobile phones, remote appliances, IoT, wearable devices
- Cloud computing services
  - Mobile devices interact with 24x7 access to cloud services
- Improved technologies
  - Reliable, safe and speedy connections
  - Management of devices (Mobile Device Management) software and capabilities

---

§ 7.7.1 Mobile Computing Benefits

- Mobile computing benefits include:
  - Tailoring to individual needs
  - Variety of access points and channels
  - Remote working
  - Capability for collaboration across virtual teams
- Mobile computing challenges include:
  - Security risks, breaches and threats; unauthorized access; lost devices
  - Power requirements, dependent on battery technology
  - Connectivity, dependency on mobile signal capability

VeriSM™ – Foundation Courseware

§ 7.7.2 | Bring Your Own Device

- Bring Your Own Device (BOYD)
  - Started with employees using their own technology at home for work purposes
  - Spread into employees accessing work information on personal devices, from email then to applications and services
  - Now includes any technologies including wearable tech, for employees to interact with the business environment
  - Traditional practices of devices controlled by the organization may be seen as a constraint

©2018 Van Haren Publishing

§ 7.7.2.1 | Bring Your Own Device Benefits

- Benefits of BOYD include:
  - Increased employee satisfaction; improved workplace flexibility and productivity; support for remote working for mobile employees; lowered capital expenditure
- Operating and Service Management risks include:
  - Security risks from compromised or lost devices, shared devices with others
  - Compliance issues (legal, regulatory and contractual)
  - Maintenance and support from the device manufacturer rather than the organization
  - Liability issues around data and information confidentiality
  - Legalities around phone number ownership and device IP address
  - Handling hacked devices that may install rogue applications onto the company network

©2018 Van Haren Publishing

§ 7.8 — Mobile Device Management

- Staff expectation, particularly GenY, of seamless blend of business and personal technology
  - Challenge is how to control assets not provisioned or controlled by the organization
- Mobile Device Management (MDM) includes:
  - Discovery, inventory, monitoring and control of employee-owned devices
  - Wiping data or selective information from devices if they are lost, stolen or the employee leaves the company
  - Setting device attributes to ensure operation within established security policies
  - Preventing devices from introducing malware into the organization
  - Establishing mechanisms for safe connection to company network and segregating the network

§ 7.9 — Serverless Computing

- Serverless computing
  - A cloud-based service model, management carried out by the supplier
  - Function-as-a-Service (FaaS) provides a platform for application functionality
  - Serverless for the organizational consumer, application based in supplier cloud
- Advantages:
  - Developer focus
  - Capacity and demand management 'owned' by supplier
  - Potential cost savings over an 'always-on server-based solution'
- Disadvantages
  - Time taken to turn on computing functions before they can be used

Artificial Intelligence

- Artificial Intelligence
  - Problem solving and decision making computing like human intelligence
  - Logic systems; Decision making systems; Speech recognition; Language translation
- Capabilities include:
  - Search algorithms using logic trees; probability theory for decision-making; pattern recognition
- Examples of AI:
  - Healthcare; Education; Personal finance; Legal firms; Manufacturing
- AI benefits include:
  - Replicating human decisions and actions; removing human limitations; powering services and products; transportation and self-drive vehicles

---

Robotic Process Automation

- Robotic Process Automation (RPA)
  - Combines Business Process Automation (BPA), task automation and AI with Machine Learning, most suited to rule based tasks
  - RPA works by configuring software to include rule sets that capture and interpret the actions of applications and individuals supporting a business process
  - Examples of use: repetitive changes; common responses; provisioning
- Benefits of RPA include:
  - Reduction in manual labor; increased processing speed; fewer errors
- Challenges of RPA include:
  - Recruitment of staff with appropriate skills; resistance from staff; problem processes

§ 7.12 — Machine Learning

- Machine Learning
  - Enable systems to learn and improve without human intervention or programming
  - Machine Learning systems use data, rule bases and Artificial Intelligence, to look for patterns to trigger changes in logic and decisions so that the behavior of systems is improved
- Learning strategies include:
  - Supervised learning
  - Unsupervised
  - Reinforcement learning

§ 7.13 — Containerization

- Containerization
  - Addresses issues encountered when applications are developed, tested and released into production
  - Breaks down applications into smaller functional components, deployed as a single unit
  - Manages differing demands; if demand increases, more containers are used
  - Containers wrap and bundle applications into a complete file system that can be deployed on any platform
  - Containerization engine abstracts the file system from the underlying operating system and hardware

Module 6

Quiz questions

- In which part of the VeriSM model can you find 'innovative or emergent technologies'?

a) Governance
b) Service management principles
c) Management Mesh
d) Activities

Module 6

Quiz questions

- In which part of the VeriSM model can you find 'innovative or emergent technologies'?

a) Governance
b) Service management principles
c) Management Mesh
d) Activities

VeriSM™ – Foundation Courseware

Quiz questions

- What do staff in an organization adopting VeriSM need to ensure when considering emerging technologies?
1. Service provider staff have the correct skills
2. The organization is always using the most recent technology
3. The knowledge requirements have been met
4. The sourcing model responsibilities are understood

a) 2, 3 & 4
b) 1, 3 & 4
c) 1, 2 & 3
d) 1, 2 & 4

Quiz questions

- What do staff in an organization adopting VeriSM need to ensure when considering emerging technologies?
1. Service provider staff have the correct skills
2. The organization is always using the most recent technology
3. The knowledge requirements have been met
4. The sourcing model responsibilities are understood

a) 2, 3 & 4
b) 1, 3 & 4
c) 1, 2 & 3
d) 1, 2 & 4

Quiz questions

- Which of these are key service management considerations for emergent technology when adopting the VeriSM model?
1. The ITIL service management processes are all in place
2. The current technical maturity level
3. The current capabilities and resources in the Management Mesh
4. A service integrator has been appointed to manage suppliers

a) 2 & 3 only
b) 1, 3 & 4
c) 1, 2 & 3
d) 1 & 4 only

Quiz questions

- Which of these are key service management considerations for emergent technology when adopting the VeriSM model?
1. The ITIL service management processes are all in place
2. The current technical maturity level
3. The current capabilities and resources in the Management Mesh
4. A service integrator has been appointed to manage suppliers

a) 2 & 3 only
b) 1, 3 & 4
c) 1, 2 & 3
d) 1 & 4 only

§ 8.1

Getting Started

- VeriSM applies service management across the whole organization
  - Re-defines teams and departments as organizational capabilities
  - Re-defines the entire organization as a service provider
- Acceptance of the new approach involves:
  - Understanding VeriSM is an organizational philosophy, not one based in IT
  - Presenting the case to the organizational leadership and gaining buy-in
  - Performing a SWOT analysis to assess the potential benefits of adopting VeriSM
- Moving to the VeriSM approach involves:
  - More than one person, it is a re-definition of the whole organization
  - Use organizational change management techniques
  - Recruit the volunteer army to define how to move forward

  ©2018 Van Haren Publishing

8.1

Review the Current State

- Examine:
  - Current Management Mesh elements – available resources, management practices, environmental factors and emerging technologies
  - Management practices and any others that might be applicable
  - Emerging technologies for exploitation
  - Organization's tactical and strategic plans
  - Organizational internal and external environments, are they changing?
  - Current operational processes, measurements and tools, and assess their contribution to service delivery

Next step: Devise a plan, based on the assessment of the Mesh, to fill any gaps

  ©2018 Van Haren Publishing

§ 8.2 — Proactive Approach

- Encourage a proactive mindset by asking:
  - Where is the organization going?
  - How well do we support the service offerings?
  - What could be done differently to achieve the organizational objectives?
- Proactive organizations will utilize continual improvement activities:
  - Reviewing services, measuring performance, working to organizational objectives
  - VeriSM supports a proactive approach

§ 8.2 — Proactive vs Reactive

- Reactive organizations are often in 'fire-fighting' mode
  - No time to carry out organizational assessment
- A proactive approach considers:
  - Are services meeting consumer needs now and in the future
  - Focus on Define and Produce activities
- Management support is essential
  - Staff move from fire-fighting to fire-prevention
  - Recognize proactive achievement as well as reactive success

Becoming Proactive

Breaking out of Fire-fighting Mode

- Lens
  Analysis

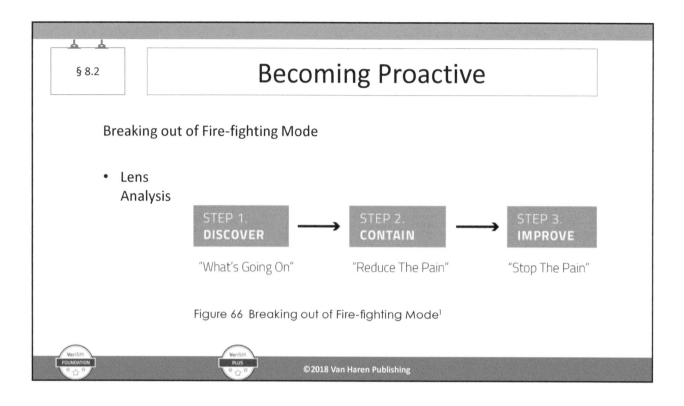

Figure 66 Breaking out of Fire-fighting Mode[1]

Acceptance of VeriSM

- What services and offerings are currently being provided to consumers?
- What is the current organizational mission and vision?
- Is there a strategy? Is it communicated?
- How are the organizational capabilities addressing the strategy?
- Is the strategy for service delivery aligned to the organizational mission and vision?
- How do the organizational capabilities contribute to the product or service offerings?

Examination Type

Examination type	: Computer-based or paper-based multiple-choice questions
Number of questions	: 40
Pass mark	: 65% (26 of 40)
Open book/notes	: No
Electronic equipment/aides permitted	: No
Time allotted for examination	: 60 minutes

The Rules and Regulations for examinations apply to this exam.

Good Luck!

Assignments VeriSM™

- These assignments are designed to get the candidate to think about the concepts of VeriSM using their own experiences and as such do not have a definitive 'correct' answer.

- They may be used as group exercises to drive discussion of the key elements covered in the assignments, or as an individual revision exercise to consolidate the course learning.

- The timings for each assignment are guidance only, and discretion should be used in the use of assignments to support the candidates learning.

Assignment Module 1 - List 5 organizations

List 5 organizations that have benefited from digital transformation and in what way?

Plan to spend 15 minutes on this assignment.

Assignment Module 2 - Elements of VeriSM

The VeriSM material shows a set of elements that make up a service culture, displayed as E^{10}

- Empathy, Excellence, Empowerment, Engagement, Easy to do business with, Everyone, Environment, Experience, Encouragement, Effective

Provide an explanation of each of these elements, using your own experience for reference.

Plan to spend 15 minutes on this assignment.

Assignment Module 3 - Leader and Manager

Explain the aspects of a Leader and Manager, and differences between the two.

Plan to spend 15 minutes on this assignment.

Assignment Module 4 - Elements of VeriSM and Management Mesh

Define the elements of the VeriSM model, and the elements of the Management Mesh.

Plan to spend 15 minutes on this assignment.

Assignment Module 5 - DevOps, Agile, Lean

Given the situations in the table below, identify which would be suitable for DevOps, Agile, Lean

Plan to spend 15 minutes on this assignment.

Situational Analysis	DevOps	Agile	Lean
Desire to eliminate in-fighting and to break silos between development and operational teams.			
Desire to eliminate operational churn, defects and errors associated with deployments.			
Products or services where business value needs to be obtained quickly.			
Products or services expected to incur rapid change after going live.			
Desire to more efficiently manage and deal with services and applications that experience a high volume of change.			
Desire to stop firefighting caused by problematic services and products.			

Assignment Module 6 - Service management

What are the service management implications for innovative technologies, list as many of these as you can from your own experience.

Plan to spend 15 minutes on this assignment.

Answer Assignment Module 1 - List 5 organizations

List 5 organizations that have benefited from digital transformation and in what way?

Plan to spend 15 minutes on this assignment.

- Reference syllabus section 1.3.1

List 5 organizations that have benefited from digital transformation and in what way?

- Examples should include organizations like Amazon, who have begun to use digital transformation and emergent technologies for not just their consumer interface (Alexa, email contact, self service etc.), but also their transportation and logistics (warehouse management, stock management and control, etc.).

- Candidates should also be able to identify digital transformation examples in their own organizations.

Answer Assignment Module 2 - Elements of VeriSM

The VeriSM material shows a set of elements that make up a service culture, displayed as E^{10}:

- Empathy, Excellence, Empowerment, Engagement, Easy to do business with, Everyone, Environment, Experience, Encouragement, Effective

Provide an explanation of each of these elements, using your own experience for reference.

Plan to spend 15 minutes on this assignment.

- Reference syllabus section 2.1.3

Below is the example given in the VeriSM Handbook, compare your answer with this.

Element	Includes
Empathy	Putting yourself in the consumer's position.
Excellence	Exceeding consumer expectations.
Empowerment	Allowing staff to act in the consumer's interests.
Engagement	Appearing approachable and personable.
Easy to do business with	Efficient, easy to contact.
Everyone	All staff understand their contribution to the whole.
Environment	Culture of the organization.
Experience	The reality of the product or service matches what was promised.
Encouragement	Service provider staff get recognition and rewards.
Effective	The service provider delivers what was promised, when it was promised.

Answer Assignment Module 3 - Leader and Manager

Explain the aspects of a Leader and Manager, and differences between the two.

Plan to spend 15 minutes on this assignment.

- Reference syllabus section 3.1.1

- This is the example given in the VeriSM Handbook

Leaders	Managers
Set goals and direction;	Resource-oriented;
Challenge the norm;	Plan, budget and organize;
Look for new ways to excel;	Maintain the status quo;
Motivate, empower and inspire.	Minimize risk;
	Focus on results.

Answer Assignment Module 4 - Elements of VeriSM and Management Mesh

Define the elements of the VeriSM model, and the elements of the Management Mesh.

Plan to spend 15 minutes on this assignment.

- Reference syllabus section 4.1.1 / 4.1.3

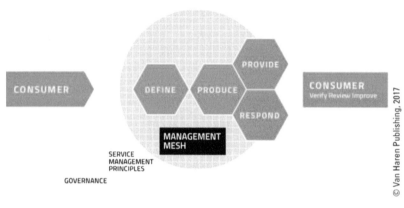

Figure 18 The VeriSM Model
Source: VeriSM™ - A service management approach for the digital age

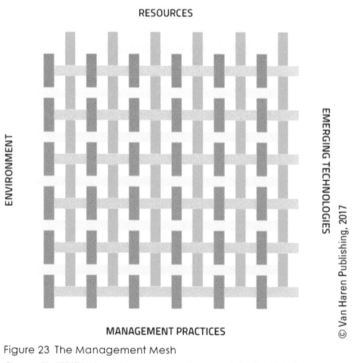

Figure 23 The Management Mesh
Source: VeriSM™ - A service management approach for the digital age

Answer Assignment Module 5 - DevOps, Agile, Lean

Given the situations in the table below, identify which would be suitable for DevOps, Agile, Lean

Plan to spend 15 minutes on this assignment.

- Reference syllabus 5.1.2

Situational Analysis	DevOps	Agile	Lean
Desire to eliminate in-fighting and to break silos between development and operational teams.	X		
Desire to eliminate operational churn, defects and errors associated with deployments.	X		
Products or services where business value needs to be obtained quickly.	X	X	X
Products or services expected to incur rapid change after going live.	X	X	X
Desire to more efficiently manage and deal with services and applications that experience a high volume of change.	X	X	X
Desire to stop firefighting caused by problematic services and products.	X		X

Answer Assignment Module 6 - Service management

What are the service management implications for innovative technologies, list as many of these as you can from your own experience.

Plan to spend 15 minutes on this assignment.

- Reference syllabus section 6.1.1

These are the examples given in the VeriSM Handbook, compare these to your own.

Service management implications:

- Identifying which emerging technologies should be adopted, technical staff may be tempted by the new and latest technology, but they may be short-lived

- There is a risk of the technology dictating the solution, rather than the consumer requirement

- Unwanted new functionality may be a waste of time and resources

- Engagement of the consumers from the start of the development, avoiding assumptions

- Develop a relationship between senior managers and consumers, ensuring the strategy remains aligned

- Learn from experience

- New technology is used to meet a requirement, not just because its new

- Service provider has the awareness, engagement and involvement from consumers to choose the best technical solutions

International Foundation for Digital Competences

Certification requirements for VeriSM™

VeriSM™ Foundation, *Essentials* and *Plus*

VeriSM™
Service Management
for the digital age

Version v180103

International Foundation for Digital Competences

Content

VeriSM™ is a registered trademark of IFDC.

1. Overview

VeriSM™ Foundation, VeriSM™ *Essentials*, and VeriSM™ *Plus*

Scope

VeriSM™ is a service management approach that helps service providers to create a flexible operating model to meet desired business outcomes. It describes how an organization can define its service management principles and then use organizational capabilities, emerging technologies and a combination of management practices to deliver value. VeriSM™ Foundation certification validates a professional's knowledge about:

- The Service Organization
- Service culture
- People and organizational structure
- The VeriSM™ model
- Progressive practices
- Innovative technologies
- Getting started.

Summary

VeriSM™ describes a service management approach from the organizational level, looking at the end to end view rather than focusing on a single department. Based around the VeriSM™ model, it shows organizations how they can adopt a range of management practices in a flexible way to deliver the right product or service at the right time to their consumers. VeriSM™ allows a tailored approach depending upon the type of business you are in, the size of your organization, your business priorities, your organizational culture, and even the nature of the individual project or service you are working on. Rather than focusing on one prescriptive way of working, it helps organizations to respond to their consumers and deliver value with integrated service management practices. VeriSM™ shows you how to fit your current, effective ways of working into an overall organizational context and flexibly adopt different management practices to meet different service management situations.

The VeriSM™ Foundation certification builds the fundamental skills and knowledge enabling individuals to participate in a service organization and to deliver value to the consumer The certification is based on VeriSM™ - A service management approach for the digital age (see Exam Literature in Chapter 4).

International Foundation for Digital Competences

Context

The VeriSM™ Foundation, VeriSM™ *Essentials* and VeriSM™ *Plus* certificates are part of the VeriSM™ qualification program.

The Foundation level can be offered in its entirety, but it has also been split up into two parts which can be offered separately as well: the VeriSM™ Essentials and the VeriSM™ Plus. The VeriSM™ Essentials focuses on the basic service management principles, where VeriSM™ Plus focuses on the progressive practices and how these relate to service management.

Target group

The target group consists of all professionals and organizations involved in delivering value to customers through the development, delivery, operation and/or promotion of services. VeriSM™ Foundation, VeriSM™ *Essentials* and VeriSM™ *Plus* prove to be useful both for professionals at the very start of their service management career and for experienced professionals who need access to a simple service management approach.

The certifications are essential for anyone who works with products and services and will be of particular interest to:

- Graduates and undergraduates – who will be joining organizations and who need to understand the principles of service management.
- Everyone within a service organization, in particular:
    - Managers – who want to understand how to leverage evolving management practices;
    - Service owners and service managers – who need to bring their skills up to date and understand how service management has changed;
    - Executives – who are accountable for effective service delivery;
    - IT professionals - who need to understand the impact of evolving management practices and new technologies on their role.

Requirements for certification

VeriSM™ Foundation

- Successful completion of the VeriSM™ Foundation exam.

VeriSM™ *Essentials*

- Successful completion of the VeriSM™ *Essentials* exam.

VeriSM™ *Plus*

- Successful completion of the VeriSM™ *Plus* exam.

The following certificates will also lead to a VeriSM™ Foundation certificate:

- A certificate in an existing Service Management certification + successful completion of the VeriSM™ *Plus* exam.
- Successful completion of the VeriSM™ *Essentials* exam + successful completion of the VeriSM™ *Plus* exam.

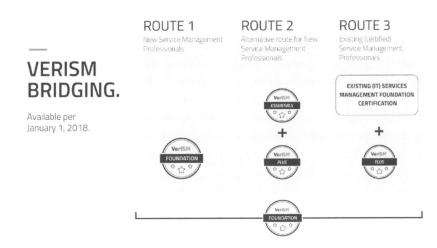

Examination details

VeriSM™ Foundation

Examination type:	Computer-based or paper-based multiple-choice questions
Number of questions:	40
Pass mark:	65% (26 out of 40)
Open book/notes:	No
Electronic equipment/aides permitted:	No
Time allotted for examination:	60 minutes

VeriSM™ *Essentials*

Examination type: Computer-based or paper-based multiple-choice questions

Number of questions: 20

Pass mark: 65% (13 out of 20)

Open book/notes: No

Electronic equipment/aides permitted: No

Time allotted for examination: 30 minutes

VeriSM™ *Plus*

Examination type: Computer-based or paper-based multiple-choice questions

Number of questions: 20

Pass mark: 65% (13 out of 20)

Open book/notes: No

Electronic equipment/aides permitted: No

Time allotted for examination: 30 minutes

Bloom level

The VeriSM™ Foundation, VeriSM™ *Essentials* and VeriSM™ *Plus* certifications test candidates at Bloom Level 1 and Level 2 according to Bloom's Revised Taxonomy:

- Bloom Level 1: Remembering – relies on recall of information. Candidates will need to absorb, remember, recognize and recall. This is the building block of learning before candidates can move on to higher levels.
- Bloom Level 2: Understanding – a step beyond remembering. Understanding shows that candidates comprehend what is presented and can evaluate how the learning material may be applied in their own environment.

Training

Contact hours

VeriSM™ Foundation

The recommended number of contact hours for this training course is 14. This includes group assignments, exam preparation and short breaks. This number of hours does not include homework, the exam session and lunch breaks.

VeriSM™ *Essentials*

The recommended number of contact hours for this training course is 7. This includes group assignments, exam preparation and short breaks. This number of hours does not include homework, the exam session and lunch breaks.

VeriSM™ *Plus*

The recommended number of contact hours for this training course is 7. This includes group assignments, exam preparation and short breaks. This number of hours does not include homework, the exam session and lunch breaks.

Indication study effort

VeriSM™ Foundation

40 hours

VeriSM™ *Essentials*

20 hours

VeriSM™ *Plus*

20 hours

Study effort is the average effort to prepare for the exam, which can differ per candidate depending on the knowledge they already have. It includes reading the literature, trying the sample exam, attending the training session.

International Foundation for Digital Competences

2. Certification requirements

The certification requirements are specified in the exam specifications. The following table lists the topics of the module (exam requirements) and the subtopics (exam specifications)

Certification requirement	Exam specification	Weight Foundation	Weight Essentials	Weight Plus
1. The Service Organization				
	1.1 Organizational context	2,5%	5%	
	1.2 Organizational governance	2,5%	5%	
	1.3 Digital transformation	5%	5%	5%
2. Service culture				
	2.1 Service culture	5%	10%	
3. People and organizational structure				
	3.1 Organization structure	10%	10%	15%
	3.2 Service Management challenges	10%	15%	
4. The VeriSM™ model				
	4.1 The VeriSM™ model	25%	50%	15%
	4.2 Adapting the VeriSM™ model	7,5%		15%
5. Progressive practices				
	5.1 Progressive practices	20%		30%
6. Innovative technologies				
	6.1 Impact of technology	10%		15%
7. Getting started				
	7.1 Getting started	2,5%		5%
	Total	100%	100%	100%

Exam specifications

The column 'Tested in:' refers to the exam Foundation (F), *Essentials* (E), *Plus* (PL).

1.	The Service Organization			Tested in:
	1.1	Organizational context		
		The candidate can···		
		1.1.1	Define key elements of an organization.	F, E
		1.1.2	Describe how to optimize organizational interactions.	F, E
	1.2	Organizational governance		
		The candidate can···		
		1.2.1	Define the elements of organizational governance (evaluate, direct, monitor).	F, E
		1.2.2	Explain how governance "flows" through an organization.	F, E
	1.3	Digital transformation		
		1.3.1	Define the impact of technology changes on organizations.	F, E, PL
		1.3.2	Describe the impact of digital transformation on service management.	F, E, PL

2.	Service culture			Tested in:
	2.1	Service culture		
		The candidate can···		
		2.1.1	Define a service culture.	F, E
		2.1.2	Explain the elements of a service culture.	F, E

3.	People and organizational structure			Tested in:
	3.1	Organization structure		
		The candidate can···		
		3.1.1	Define the differences between a leader and a manager.	F, E, PL
		3.1.2	Explain the competencies of the service management professional.	F, E, PL
		3.1.3	List the elements of a well-functioning team.	F, E, PL
	3.2	Service Management challenges		
		The candidate can···		
		3.2.1	Explain methods to overcome team challenges (silos, virtual teams).	F, E

International Foundation for Digital Competences

		3.2.2	Explain the challenges of managing consumers.	F, E
		3.2.3	Describe the elements of communication.	F, E
		3.2.4	Explain organizational change principles.	F, E

4.	**The VeriSM™ model**			**Tested in:**
	4.1	**The VeriSM™ model**		
		The candidate can⋯		
		4.1.1	Define the elements of the VeriSM™ model.	F, E, PL
		4.1.2	Explain how VeriSM™ re-defines service management.	F, E, PL
		4.1.3	Explain how VeriSM™ uses the management mesh to create and support services.	F, E, PL
		4.1.4	Explain the elements within each of the four stages of the VeriSM™ Model: • Define • Produce • Provide • Respond	F, E, PL
	4.2	**Adapting the VeriSM™ model**		
		The candidate can⋯		
		4.2.1	Define the process of selecting and integrating management practices.	F, PL
		4.2.2	Explain the characteristics of successful operating models.	F, PL

5.	**Progressive practices**			**Tested in:**
	5.1	**Progressive practices**		
		The candidate can⋯		
		5.1.1	Indicate the success factors for adopting progressive management practices.	F, PL
		5.1.2	Clarify the key concepts and when to apply Agile, DevOps, SIAM, Lean as a management practice.	F, PL
		5.1.3	Define the importance of considering Shift Left, Customer Experience/User Experience, Continuous Delivery practices in service delivery.	F, PL

6.	**Innovative technologies**			**Tested in:**
	6.1	**Impact of technology**		

		The candidate can⋯	
		6.1.1	Summarize the implications of technology on service management.	F, PL
		6.1.2	Explain the benefits of cloud, virtualization, and automation.	F, PL
		6.1.3	Explain the impact of big data, internet of things, mobile computing, bring your own device on service management.	F, PL
		6.1.4	Define serverless computing, artificial intelligence, Robotic Process Automation (RPA), Machine Learning, and containerization in relation to service delivery.	F, PL

7.	Getting started			Tested in:
	7.1	**Getting started**		
		The candidate can⋯		
		7.1.1	Identify steps to initiate an improvement program based on VeriSM™.	F, PL
		7.1.2	Differentiate between reactive and proactive operations.	F, PL

3.   List of Basic Concepts

This chapter contains the terms and abbreviations with which candidates should be familiar.

Please note that knowledge of these terms alone does not suffice for the exam; the candidate must understand the concepts and be able to provide examples.

Agile service management	Network effect
A-shaped professional	Operant behavior
Asset	Operation model
Behavior	Operational planning
Best practice	Organization
Business model	Organizational behavior management (OBM)
Business relationship management	Organizational capability
Business service management	Outcome
Capability	Output
Change	PESTEL
Change fatigue	Policy
Competence, -ies	Principle
Consumer	Problem
Consumer experience	Procedure
Continuous delivery	Process
Continuous deployment	Product
Continuous integration	Profession
Contract management	Provider
Critical thinking	Quality
Culture	Reflective practice
Customer	Relationship management
Customer experience (CX)	Request
Customer relationship management	Retrospective
Cybersecurity	Role
Data protection	Service
DevOps	Service culture
Digital disruption	Service integration and management (SIAM)
Digital native	Service management
Digital optimization	Service management operating model
Digital service	Service provider
Digital transformation	Shadow behavior
Enterprise service management	Shadow IT
Expectation management	Silo
Explicit knowledge	Skills inventory
Financial management	Solution
Implicit knowledge	Source event
Incident	Stakeholder
Information Security	Stand-up meeting
I-shaped professional	Strategic planning
Issue	Supplier management
Knowledge Management	SWOT
Lifelong learning	Tacit knowledge
Management	Tactical planning
Management practices	Target operating model
Mission	Team

Technical debt	Value proposition
Tribalism	Values
T-shaped professional	VeriSM™
User	VeriSM™ Model including: - Governance - Service Management Principles - Management mesh - Define - Produce - Provide - Respond
User experience (UX)	Virtual team
Value	Vision

4.   Literature

Exam Literature

A   Title : VeriSM™ - A service management approach for the digital age

Authors: Claire Agutter, Rob England, Suzanne D. Van Hove, Randy Steinberg

Van Haren Publishing: December 2017

ISBN hard copy : 978 94 018 0240 6

ISBN eBook : 978 94 018 0241 3

Literature reference

Exam requirement	Exam specification	Literature	Literature reference
1	1.1	A	Chapter 1, §2.1 - 2.4
	1.2	A	§2.5
	1.3	A	Chapter 3, 16
2	2.1	A	Chapter 4
3	3.1	A	Chapter 5
	3.2	A	Chapter 6
4	4.1	A	Chapter 7, 8, 9, 10, 11, 12, 13, 14
	4.2	A	Chapter 11, 15
5	5.1	A	Chapter 17, 18, 19, 20, 21, 22, 23, 24
6	6.1	A	Chapter 25
7	7.1	A	Chapter 26

Page 14 of 15

158

International Foundation for Digital Competences

www.ifdc.global

The IFDC has approved APMG, BCS and EXIN as official Exam Institutes for VeriSM™ certification worldwide as from January 1st, 2018. The Exam Institutes will plan localizations (translations) where there is a market need in a specific region which relies on local language exams.

Official Publisher of the VeriSM™ Official Publications is Van Haren Publishing.

VeriSM™ Foundation Sample Exam

1

Introduction

This is the sample exam VeriSM™ Foundation.

This exam consists of 40 multiple-choice questions. Each multiple-choice question has a number of possible answers, of which only one is the correct answer.

The maximum number of points that can be obtained for this exam is 40. Each correct answer is worth one point. If you obtain 26 points or more you will pass.

The time allowed for this exam is 60 minutes.

Good luck!

2

Sample exam

1 / 40
What is the **best** description of shadow behavior?

A) A junior observing a senior by doing job-shadowing and learning on-the-job
B) Creating a tribal system where team members are overshadowed by others
C) Implementing systems or solutions without explicit organizational approval
D) IT service provisioning being so good that consumers are unaware of IT

2 / 40
How does governance flow through an organization?

A) Via delegation from owners to a governing body, who authorize organizational capabilites to take actions to create and support the outcomes to consumers.
B) Via good planning in the higher levels of the organization, where it is critical that there is a clearly stated mission and vision with key objectives defined.
C) Via organization-wide gatherings once or twice a year, where owners/stakeholders present the mission, vision and objectives, and take feedback from employees.
D) Via performance contracts between an employee and his or her manager, making everybody responsible for part of the strategy.

3 / 40
New technology has led to changes within organizations.

Which is one of these changes?

A) Services are driven by stable management practices which discourage technology innovation.
B) Services can be delivered from anywhere to anywhere.
C) Services now undergo a more rigid functional change approach within organizations.
D) Services that rely on traditional rigid management approaches are preferable to organizations.

3

Document version: v221217

4 / 40

Digital transformation requires a new approach to service management within organizations.

Where is the ownership of service management principles situated in an organization?

A) Business owns service management.
B) IT owns service management.
C) Service management is outsourced to a third-party supplier.
D) Service management is owned across the whole organization.

5 / 40

How can organizational culture **best** be described?

A) It is a collection of common practices based on the backgrounds of all employees within an organization.
B) It is a reflection of the ethnicity of management and owners within an organization.
C) It is a culture that is exclusively defined by the leadership of an organization.
D) It is a collection of, and interaction between, the values, systems, symbols, assumptions, beliefs and habits of an organization.

6 / 40

What is the **most** important element of creating a service culture?

A) Empowering the employees to make decisions on their own
B) Measuring the service culture in order to identify improvement ideas
C) Showing the consumer that they are valued by actions rather then telling them
D) Training employees and managers in good service behavior

7 / 40

What is the key activity of a leader's role?

A) Focus on results
B) Minimize risk
C) Motivate colleagues
D) Set up priorities

4

Document version: v221217

8 / 40

Emotional intelligence defines two main competencies: personal and social.

Which two skills belong to the social competence?

A) Joining social groups and actively communicating with them
B) Knowing social media and what people or situations can influence us
C) Social awareness and relationship management
D) Social content management and using social techniques

9 / 40

What is the name of the professional that should have both breadth and depth of knowledge?

A) A-shaped professional
B) I-shaped professional
C) Service management expert
D) T-shaped professional

10 / 40

What is the **last** stage of team formation?

A) Adjourning
B) Forming
C) Performing
D) Setting-up

11 / 40

There is a challenge that teams may operate in silos.

What is a recommendation that management should do to overcome this challenge?

A) Implement one-on-one meetings between team members
B) Provide team-building activities for each team
C) Reward teams who achieve their goals ahead of target
D) Share information on the organization's strategies

5

12 / 40

Successful expectation management depends on developing a clear vision of what is expected.

How can this clarity be achieved?

A) Ensure that detailed SLA documentation is available
B) Report achievement against agreed targets
C) Set boundaries and provide a structure for delivery
D) Under-promise and over-deliver

13 / 40

What is one of the five components that should be considered in communication?

A) Delivery mechanism
B) Intention
C) Perception
D) Scope

14 / 40

What is the **first** important step in the Kotter's Organizational Change Management (OCM) model?

A) Build a guiding coalition
B) Create a sense of urgency
C) Generate short-term wins
D) Institute change

15 / 40

Which element of the VeriSM™ model defines the management activities or practices necessary to meet the governance requirements by providing guardrails or boundaries?

A) Define
B) Management Mesh
C) Produce
D) Service management principles

6

Following the deployment of a new product or service, the service provider will provide ongoing support in its use to consumers.

Which element of the VeriSM™ model describes this provision of support?

A) Define
B) Produce
C) Provide
D) Respond

What is the **main** reason VeriSM™ re-defines traditional service management?

A) VeriSM™ divides service management within an organization into separate entities so all entities can work autonomously.
B) VeriSM™ focuses on the big picture and does not provide practices for specific organizations.
C) VeriSM™ incorporates new technologies and therefore helps IT departments with digital transformation.
D) VeriSM™ regards the entire organization as the service provider with capabilities that work together.

What differentiates VeriSM™ from other IT service management approaches?

A) VeriSM™ differentiates IT from other service management practices.
B) VeriSM™ focuses on the corporate IT aspects in the organization.
C) VeriSM™ is a logical evolution to older IT service management practices.
D) VeriSM™ takes all organizational capabilities into account.

VeriSM™ introduces the concept of the Management Mesh. This combines the four elements of resources, management practices, environment and emerging technologies to create and deliver products and services.

In which element should frameworks such as ITIL or methodologies such as COBIT be included?

A) Emerging technologies
B) Environment
C) Management practices
D) Resources

7

Document version: v221217

20 / 40

The Management Mesh can only be built once the organizational governance and service management principles are understood.

What else must also be developed before the Mesh is built?

A) Design specifications
B) Operational plans
C) Strategic plans
D) Tactical plans

21 / 40

What is an objective of the Define stage in the VeriSM™ model?

A) To address activities and supporting outcomes that relate to the design of a product or service
B) To ensure the product or service is available for consumption
C) To react to service issues, inquiries and requests from the consumer
D) To take the service blueprint and perform build, test and implement activities under change control

22 / 40

Why is testing an important part of the Produce stage?

A) To define risk criteria and the risk appetite of an organization
B) To ensure that the product or service meets the requirements set
C) To ensure that the organization's requirements are in line with its strategy
D) To ensure an organization's architecture is appropriate

23 / 40

What activity is part of the Provide stage?

A) Build
B) Design
C) Improve
D) Test

24 / 40

What is covered by the activity Record in the Respond stage?

A) Capture information
B) Deliver results
C) Resolve the issue
D) Source events

8

25 / 40

What steps describe the high-level process for adapting the VeriSM™ model?

A) Define the stakeholders, select the processes, and implement them in the organization
B) Establish the principles, select a set of practices, create a responsive operating model
C) Investigate all practices in use, select the best set, and make these mandatory
D) Select the best management practice, focus thereon, and implement it step by step

26 / 40

The Define stage of the VeriSM™ model produces a definition of what good service looks like.

During which process does this activity take place?

A) Create the service blueprint
B) Create the solution
C) Define consumer needs
D) Gather requirements

27 / 40

Which is the objective of service measurement?

A) To demonstrate compliance with laws, regulations and contractual commitments
B) To enable service providers to manage the performance capabilities of underpinning service elements
C) To enable the consumer to understand the costs of providing the service
D) To quantify and qualify the results or outcomes provided by a service

28 / 40

An organization is growing rapidly and therefore wants to reconsider all their processes. They find that testing is too risky. They want to minimize costs of fixing errors resulting from late discovery of integration and test errors.

Which management practice would **best** address this issue?

A) Agile
B) CX/UX
C) Lean
D) SIAM

9

29 / 40

How can Agile be used to support service management?

A) Agile cannot be used as it is a project management-only practice
B) For building products and services iteratively
C) For easy acceptance of all service management practices across the entire organization
D) To build all service management processes like traditional waterfall projects

30 / 40

How does DevOps advance service management practices?

A) DevOps advances service management practices by shifting them to the left, making them leaner.
B) DevOps sets up the principles for service management practices.
C) DevOps should be used only to develop new products and services.
D) DevOps was established later than service management and therefore does not advance service management practices.

31 / 40

What is the third layer between consumer and provider in Service and Integration Management (SIAM)?

A) Service advocate
B) Service installer
C) Service integrator
D) Service manager

32 / 40

In Lean, different types of waste are distinguished.

What type of waste is "producing at levels of quality more than required by the customer"?

A) Inventory
B) Overdelivering
C) Overprocessing
D) Overproduction

10

33 / 40

Shift Left is an approach which sees solution development, delivery and support pushed to earlier stages in their lifecycle and so gains efficiencies, cost savings and improved customer focus.

Which activity is **not** a feature of Shift Left?

A) Auto-correction of operational issues after they have occurred
B) Auto-detection of potential operational issues before they occur
C) Automatic incident referral to second line support
D) Self service incident diagnosis

34 / 40

What is the **first** step in building a customer journey map?

A) Define
B) Investigate
C) Plan
D) Research

35 / 40

How does continuous delivery **positively** impact change control processes?

A) It does not impact the change control processes.
B) It impacts the processes through automated testing facilities.
C) It impacts the processes through delivering more information.
D) It impacts the processes through less rigorous change control.

36 / 40

Technology is changing fast and this provides significant challenges for service management.

What is a generic challenge identified for service management?

A) Ensuring cost is matched to budget
B) Matching expectations to business relationships
C) More complexity and less visibility
D) Service management approaches support constraints

11

37 / 40
What is a **key** benefit of cloud?

A) Enhanced internal communication
B) Increased quality of the infrastructure
C) Increased speed of infrastructure service
D) Reduced operating risks

38 / 40
An organization decides to use a SaaS solution to control their new Internet of Things (IoT) monitoring devices.

What is **most** important to consider from a service management point of view?

A) A key requirement is that IoT devices have unique identifiers and IP addresses.
B) IoT services provide better behavior tracking to support real-time marketing.
C) It is an outsourced service, so no specific considerations are required.
D) The guardrails for the services must be respected also for SaaS solutions.

39 / 40
What is the advantage of Robotic Process Automation (RPA) in service management processes?

A) RPA automates tasks and therefore will always reduce headcount.
B) RPA helps in enabling employees to perform more complex tasks.
C) RPA increases the quality of the produced products as it automates tasks.
D) RPA is a manufacturing technique which cannot be used effectively in service management.

40 / 40
An organization wants to break out of fire-fighting mode and move to the proactive mode.

On which element(s) of the VeriSM™ model should the focus be **first**?

A) Define and Produce
B) Governance
C) Management Mesh
D) Provide and Respond

12

Answer key

1 / 40

What is the **best** description of shadow behavior?

A) A junior observing a senior by doing job-shadowing and learning on-the-job

B) Creating a tribal system where team members are overshadowed by others

C) Implementing systems or solutions without explicit organizational approval

D) IT service provisioning being so good that consumers are unaware of IT

A) Incorrect. Although job-shadowing is a valid skills development approach which yields good results, it has no bearing on shadow behavior. Shadow behavior is about things such as the introduction of systems into the live environment without approval.

B) Incorrect. VeriSM™ removes the barriers and tribalism found in many organizations. Overshadowing other team members is considered undesirable behavior and should be avoided according to VeriSM ™, but shadow behavior focusses on the lack of explicit organizational approval for changes in organizations.

C) Correct. Shadow behavior and specifically shadow IT is a big problem in organizations. Not following organizational approval processes and procedures (change management) introduces unknown risks into the environment and may well have an impact on the performance of other IT services. (Literature: A, Chapter 2.3.1)

D) Incorrect. It is a good thing if IT services are seen as non-intrusive and if services forms part of the functioning of the organization. However shadow behavior is not positive as it means things such as systems being implemented without approval and thereby increasing risk.

13

How does governance flow through an organization?

A) Via delegation from owners to a governing body, who authorize organizational capabilites to take actions to create and support the outcomes to consumers.

B) Via good planning in the higher levels of the organization, where it is critical that there is a clearly stated mission and vision with key objectives defined.

C) Via organization-wide gatherings once or twice a year, where owners/stakeholders present the mission, vision and objectives, and take feedback from employees.

D) Via performance contracts between an employee and his or her manager, making everybody responsible for part of the strategy.

A) Correct. There needs to be an actual frame of delegation and authorization supporting the flow of governance for it to really work. (Literature: A, Chapter 2.5.2)

B) Incorrect. Although strategic planning in the higher levels of the organization is important, it cannot be considered the backbone of how the governance flows. It will flow via delegation to a governing body, who will authorize the organizational capabilites to take action based on the mission, vision and objectives.

C) Incorrect. Although openness and invitation to dialogue from owners/stakeholders about the mission, vision and objectives may be advised, it cannot be considered the backbone of how the governance flows. It will flow via delegation to a governing body, who will authorize the organizational capabilites to take action based on the mission, vision and objectives.

D) Incorrect. Although having commitments between a manager and an employee is a good idea to ensure that everybody understands, and is accountable for their contribution to the mission, vision and objectives of the organization, there needs to be an equally strong commitment and accountability between the owners/stakeholders, who make the mission, vision and objectives, and a governing body. Who then in turn authorizes for instance managers to bring the mission, vision and objectives to life.

14

New technology has led to changes within organizations.

Which is one of these changes?

A) Services are driven by stable management practices which discourage technology innovation.

B) Services can be delivered from anywhere to anywhere.

C) Services now undergo a more rigid functional change approach within organizations.

D) Services that rely on traditional rigid management approaches are preferable to organizations.

A) Incorrect. Although stability is still important, the speed of technology change requires greater innovation, not less.

B) Correct. New innovative technologies have allowed services to be delivered from anywhere, to anywhere. (Literature: A, Chapter 3.1)

C) Incorrect. Agile approaches provide the desired flexibility, rather than rigid management.

D) Incorrect. Organizations are looking for more Agile and flexible approaches to service management, to cater for a fast changing environment.

4 / 40

Digital transformation requires a new approach to service management within organizations.

Where is the ownership of service management principles situated in an organization?

A) Business owns service management.

B) IT owns service management.

C) Service management is outsourced to a third-party supplier.

D) Service management is owned across the whole organization.

15

A) Incorrect. IT capabilities in service management need to blend in with those of other capability areas like human resources, sales, marketing, or finance, not be in the sole ownership of the business.

B) Incorrect. With digital transformation, service management can no longer be the sole property of the IT capability.

C) Incorrect. Service management is an enterprise wide approach, and should not be solely outsourced to a third party.

D) Correct. Products and services require input from multiple business capabilities who must all work together to achieve organizational objectives. Service management is elevated to the enterprise level. (Literature: A, Chapter 3.5)

5 / 40

How can organizational culture **best** be described?

A) It is a collection of common practices based on the backgrounds of all employees within an organization.

B) It is a reflection of the ethnicity of management and owners within an organization.

C) It is a culture that is exclusively defined by the leadership of an organization.

D) It is a collection of, and interaction between, the values, systems, symbols, assumptions, beliefs and habits of an organization.

16

Document version: v221217

A) Incorrect. VeriSM™ defines organizational culture as "the collection of written and unwritten rules, guidelines and practices that shape the behaviors of the people in an organization". The answer may seem correct but to say that common practices based on employee backgrounds is not correct. Employees certainly influence organizational culture but it is only one of many factors that influence culture.

B) Incorrect. Although the context in which an organization operates and managers' and owners' backgrounds influence organizational culture, a number of other factors do too. Cultural references from one group of organizational stakeholders should not form the exclusive basis of organizational culture.

C) Incorrect. The leadership of an organization certainly has a major influence on and may actively affect organizational culture, but it is by no means the only determining factor. Leaders and managers that attempt organizational change that opposes organizational culture will soon find out that this is a difficult and sometimes dangerous task and they will mostly see their change initiatives fail.

D) Correct. Culture is 'the way we do things in an organization'. According to VeriSM™ a good description would be "the collective values, systems, symbols, assumptions, beliefs and habits of an organization". All of these can be observed in how things are done in the organization. Culture is often not formally defined, written down or taught to new employees. They will mostly "observe and learn how things are done here". (Literature: A, Chapter 2.4)

6 / 40

What is the **most** important element of creating a service culture?

A) Empowering the employees to make decisions on their own

B) Measuring the service culture in order to identify improvement ideas

C) Showing the consumer that they are valued by actions rather then telling them

D) Training employees and managers in good service behavior

17

A) Incorrect. Although empowerment is one of the areas senior management needs to focus on in order to bring about a service culture, it is not the most important element of a service culture. Actually showing the consumer that they are valued by actions rather than just telling them they are valued, is the most important element though.

B) Incorrect. In order to know whether you are doing a good job, it is important to measure your performance. However, it is not the most critical element in bringing about a service culture as such. Actually showing the consumer that they are valued by actions rather than just telling them they are valued, is the most important element though.

C) Correct. Making the consumer feel that they are valued is the most important element of a service culture. (Literature: A, Chapter 4.4)

D) Incorrect. In order to bring about a service culture in an organization, it is important that employees and management are actually enabled to do so, and to spot good behavior when they see it (or when they do not). Actually showing the consumer that they are valued by actions rather than just telling them they are valued, is the most important element of creating a service culture though.

7 / 40

What is the key activity of a leader's role?

A) Focus on results

B) Minimize risk

C) Motivate colleagues

D) Set up priorities

A) Incorrect. This is a key activity of the role of a manager.

B) Incorrect. This is a key activity of the role of a manager.

C) Correct. This activity is a key characteristic that is connected with the role of a leader in VeriSM™. Other key characteristics are empower and inspire. (Literature: A, Chapter 5.1)

D) Incorrect. This is a key activity of a Product Owner in a Scrum project.

18

Emotional intelligence defines two main competencies: personal and social.

Which two skills belong to the social competence?

A) Joining social groups and actively communicating with them

B) Knowing social media and what people or situations can influence us

C) Social awareness and relationship management

D) Social content management and using social techniques

A) Incorrect. Joining social groups and communication between group members are activities not skills.

B) Incorrect. Knowing social media is not enough to express it as a skill. Knowing what people and situations can influence ourselves is a skill that belongs to the personal competence.

C) Correct. Social awareness and relationship management are two skills defined by Travis Bradberry and Jean Greaves in their work "Emotional Intelligence 2.0". (Literature: A, Chapter 5.3)

D) Incorrect. Social content management and using social techniques are not skills. Techniques are the use of specific tools, a set of rules of conduct, and skills are immanent, acquired during the learning process and growth. Techniques are how to do something, skills are how to know and understand something.

19

Document version: v221217

What is the name of the professional that should have both breadth and depth of knowledge?

A) A-shaped professional

B) I-shaped professional

C) Service management expert

D) T-shaped professional

A) Incorrect. An A-shaped professional develops expertise in two specialties.

B) Incorrect. An I-shaped professional is focused on a specific area and has great depth of information and knowledge within that area.

C) Incorrect. Service management expert is a certification, not a theory, which focuses on a particular knowledge area and depth only.

D) Correct. T-shaped professional is an innovative and powerful problem-solver in their area of expertise and capable of interacting and understanding specialists across a wide range of capabilities. (Literature: A, Chapter 5.5)

10 / 40

What is the **last** stage of team formation?

A) Adjourning

B) Forming

C) Performing

D) Setting-up

20

A) Correct. This is the last stage in the formation of a team. It is when group tasks are complete and the team disbands. The other four stages are forming, storming, norming, and performing. (Literature: A, Chapter 5.7.1)

B) Incorrect. This is the first stage in a team formation. It focuses on getting to know each other and understand the purpose of the team.

C) Incorrect. This is the fourth stage in the formation of a team. During this stage relationships, team practices and effectiveness are synced and the real work of the team is now progressing.

D) Incorrect. This is not a stage in a team formation.

11 / 40

There is a challenge that teams may operate in silos.

What is a recommendation that management should do to overcome this challenge?

A) Implement one-on-one meetings between team members

B) Provide team-building activities for each team

C) Reward teams who achieve their goals ahead of target

D) Share information on the organization's strategies

A) Incorrect. Such meetings are helpful in building a team spirit across a virtual team, but may encourage the development of silos, by encouraging the team to look inwards.

B) Incorrect. Team building activities for each team will encourage team spirit, but not collaboration with other teams.

C) Incorrect. Rewarding teams for achieving goals ahead of target may emphasize competition and discourage collaboration with other teams.

D) Correct. Sharing the organization's strategic aims will help to focus the teams on the bigger picture, so that the team works to help to achieve the overall objective. (Literature: A, Chapter 6.1)

21

Successful expectation management depends on developing a clear vision of what is expected.

How can this clarity be achieved?

A) Ensure that detailed SLA documentation is available

B) Report achievement against agreed targets

C) Set boundaries and provide a structure for delivery

D) Under-promise and over-deliver

A) Incorrect. Detailed documentation may not necessarily improve clarity, if it is overly complex or ambiguous. Service level agreements must be clear and state the level of service to be provided and how this is to be measured.

B) Incorrect. There is a danger that targets may be met, but the overall perception of the end-to-end service is poor, if the targets are not aligned to the business requirement. This is known as the watermelon effect (green on the outside, red on the inside).

C) Correct. Defining the scope of what is to be delivered in an unambiguous way will ensure that all parties are in agreement and prevent a mismatch between expectations and delivery. (Literature: A, Chapter 6.2.1)

D) Incorrect. The ambition to under-promise and then deliver a better service than agreed does not help clarify expectations, and may even raise expectations to an achievable level over time, as there is no clear agreement on what the service provider is able to provide.

22

Document version: v221217

What is one of the five components that should be considered in communication?

A) Delivery mechanism

B) Intention

C) Perception

D) Scope

A) Correct. In good communication there are five components to consider. These five components are: sender, context, receiver, delivery mechanism and content. (Literature: A, Chapter 6.4)

B) Incorrect. Intention is not one of the five components to consider in communication. Every message should have a defined purpose (intent) that the sender wants to achieve with the communication.

C) Incorrect. Perception is not one of the five components to consider in communication. It is how the message is understood.

D) Incorrect. Scope is not one of the five components to consider in communication. The scope is a part of a defined communication plan.

14 / 40

What is the **first** important step in the Kotter's Organizational Change Management (OCM) model?

A) Build a guiding coalition

B) Create a sense of urgency

C) Generate short-term wins

D) Institute change

23

A) Incorrect. This is the second stage in the model of Kotter. This stage focuses on creating the volunteer army with effective people who can guide, coordinate and communicate.

B) Correct. This is the first stage in the model of Kotter. It focuses on using opportunities that will appeal (emotionally and intellectually) to the volunteer army to urgently act. (Literature: A Chapter 6.6.1)

C) Incorrect. This is the sixth stage in the model of Kotter. It focuses on collecting and categorizing the short-term wins to show the achievement of tangible business results.

D) Incorrect. This is the last stage in the model of Kotter. It focuses on linking new behaviors to the success of the organization.

15 / 40

Which element of the VeriSM™ model defines the management activities or practices necessary to meet the governance requirements by providing guardrails or boundaries?

A) Define

B) Management Mesh

C) Produce

D) Service management principles

24

A) Incorrect. The Define stage is concerned with the activities and supporting outcomes that relate to the design of a product or service. The Define stage works within the guardrails provided by the service management principles.

B) Incorrect. The Management Mesh does not provide the guardrails; it allows teams to work on products and services flexibly, combining resources, practices, environment and emerging technologies.

C) Incorrect. The Produce stage is concerned with the creation of the solution, ensuring the outcome meets the needs of the consumer. The Produce stage works within the guardrails provided by the service management principles.

D) Correct. The service management principles are based on the organizational governing principles. They provide the guardrails for the products and services delivered, addressing areas such as quality and risk. (Literature: A, Chapter 7 and Chapter 9.1)

16 / 40

Following the deployment of a new product or service, the service provider will provide ongoing support in its use to consumers.

Which element of the VeriSM™ model describes this provision of support?

A) Define

B) Produce

C) Provide

D) Respond

25

A) Incorrect. The Define stage is concerned with the activities and supporting outcomes that relate to the design of a product or service.

B) Incorrect. The Produce stage is concerned with the creation of the solution, ensuring the outcome meets the needs of the consumer.

C) Incorrect. The Provide stage is concerned with making the new or changed solution available for use.

D) Correct. The Respond stage describes the support the consumer receives during performance issues, questions or any other requests. (Literature: A, Chapter 7 and 14.1)

17 / 40

What is the **main** reason VeriSM™ re-defines traditional service management?

A) VeriSM™ divides service management within an organization into separate entities so all entities can work autonomously.

B) VeriSM™ focuses on the big picture and does not provide practices for specific organizations.

C) VeriSM™ incorporates new technologies and therefore helps IT departments with digital transformation.

D) VeriSM™ regards the entire organization as the service provider with capabilities that work together.

A) Incorrect. VeriSM™ has a holistic view for the whole organization and it does not separate an organization into entities.

B) Incorrect. VeriSM™ provides a Mesh to personalize service management for a specific organization.

C) Incorrect. This is true, but not the main reason why it re-defines service management.

D) Correct. This is the key differentiator between VeriSM™ and ITSM. (Literature: A, Chapter 9.2)

26

What differentiates VeriSM™ from other IT service management approaches?

A) VeriSM™ differentiates IT from other service management practices.

B) VeriSM™ focuses on the corporate IT aspects in the organization.

C) VeriSM™ is a logical evolution to older IT service management practices.

D) VeriSM™ takes all organizational capabilities into account.

A) Incorrect. VeriSM™ regards all departments and area's as capabilities in delivering consumer services.

B) Incorrect. VeriSM™ focuses on the whole organization, not just IT.

C) Incorrect. VeriSM™ is the next step, but has a broader focus then traditional IT service management.

D) Correct. VeriSM™ has a holistic view over the organization as a whole. The entire organization is the service provider and the individual departments are the capabilities that support the organization as it delivers products and services. (Literature: A, Chapter 9.2)

VeriSM™ introduces the concept of the Management Mesh. This combines the four elements of resources, management practices, environment and emerging technologies to create and deliver products and services.

In which element should frameworks such as ITIL or methodologies such as COBIT be included?

A) Emerging technologies

B) Environment

C) Management practices

D) Resources

27

A) Incorrect. Emerging technologies are the advances in overall technologies such as cloud services, automation and the Internet of Things which may be exploited when designing and delivering a service.

B) Incorrect. The environmental aspects include the organizational culture, market position, and regulatory framework.

C) Correct. The management practices element of the Mesh includes frameworks such as ITIL, and methodologies such as COBIT, SIAM and DevOps. The organization chooses which to use, dependent on the requirement. (Literature: A: Chapter 10)

D) Incorrect. Resources are the elements an organization draws on to create products and services, such as people, money and assets.

20 / 40

The Management Mesh can only be built once the organizational governance and service management principles are understood.

What else must also be developed before the Mesh is built?

A) Design specifications

B) Operational plans

C) Strategic plans

D) Tactical plans

28

A) Incorrect. The Management Mesh is used to develop and deliver products and services. The design specifications are developed using the Management Mesh.

B) Incorrect. Operational plans are developed following the building of the Management Mesh. Based on the requirements, the service provider chooses the best elements for the Mesh to create the operational plan.

C) Correct. Working within the guardrails set by the organizational governance and service management principles, the service provider develops their strategic plans to address consumer requirements. Based on these, the Management Mesh is built. (Literature: A, Chapter 10.5)

D) Incorrect. Tactical plans are developed following the building of the Management Mesh. Based on the requirements, the service provider chooses the best elements for the Mesh to create the tactical plan.

21 / 40

What is an objective of the Define stage in the VeriSM™ model?

A) To address activities and supporting outcomes that relate to the design of a product or service

B) To ensure the product or service is available for consumption

C) To react to service issues, inquiries and requests from the consumer

D) To take the service blueprint and perform build, test and implement activities under change control

A) Correct. Define is about addressing the activities relating to the design of a service or product. (Literature: A, Chapter 11.1)

B) Incorrect. This is an objective for the Provide stage of the VeriSM™ model.

C) Incorrect. This is an objective for the Respond stage of the VeriSM™ model.

D) Incorrect. This is an objective for the Produce stage of the VeriSM™ model.

29

Why is testing an important part of the Produce stage?

A) To define risk criteria and the risk appetite of an organization

B) To ensure that the product or service meets the requirements set

C) To ensure that the organization's requirements are in line with its strategy

D) To ensure an organization's architecture is appropriate

A) Incorrect. The organizational appetite for risk is the responsibility of governance structures and risk criteria associated to a product of service are defined during the Define stage. Testing needs to make sure that the introduction of a new or changed service or product meets the requirements set with regards to risk and not to define what these requirements are.

B) Correct. Testing needs to ensure that the product or service meets the requirements set in the Design stage. This may include a number of tests that checks, for instance, if the product or service will meet the stakeholder needs that prompted the development of the product or service. Checking whether a service or product meets requirements set in the Define stage normally include activities like testing functionality, usability, technical compatibility etcetera, but testing should also ensure that the product or service enables business outcomes and facilitate the realization of business value. (Literature: A, Chapter 7 and Chapter 12.5)

C) Incorrect. Validating whether organizational requirements support the organization's strategy is the responsibility of the governing body and management and not the objective of testing. However, the VeriSM™ model may provide valuable feedback to management and governance structures to that end.

D) Incorrect. Evaluating the appropriateness of organizational architecture is a management activity. Testing should ensure that products and services are aligned with the defined organizational architecture and not the other way around.

30

What activity is part of the Provide stage?

A) Build

B) Design

C) Improve

D) Test

A) Incorrect. Build is a part of the Produce stage of the VeriSM™ Model. Build turns the service blueprint produced in the Define stage into actionable plans and then into action that produce the new or changed service.

B) Incorrect. It is not a part of the Provide stage. Design is not an activity of the Define stage of the VeriSM™ model but could rather be seen as a partial description of what is done in the Define stage, especially during requirements outcome, solution and the service blueprint activities.

C) Correct. Improve is an activity of the Provide stage of the VeriSM™ model. Improve includes maintenance and improvement activities. (Literature: A, Chapter 13.2)

D) Incorrect. Test is part of the Produce stage and ensures that the product or service is tested according to the designed plans. These tests should cover a variety of circumstances and will be based on organizational governance.

24 / 40

What is covered by the activity Record in the Respond stage?

A) Capture information

B) Deliver results

C) Resolve the issue

D) Source events

A) Correct. Capturing information is covered by the Record activity. (Literature: A, Chapter 14.2)

B) Incorrect. Delivering results is covered by the Manage activity.

C) Incorrect. Resolving issues is covered by the Manage activity.

D) Incorrect. Sourcing events is covered by the Manage activity.

25 / 40

What steps describe the high-level process for adapting the VeriSM™ model?

A) Define the stakeholders, select the processes, and implement them in the organization

B) Establish the principles, select a set of practices, create a responsive operating model

C) Investigate all practices in use, select the best set, and make these mandatory

D) Select the best management practice, focus thereon, and implement it step by step

A) Incorrect. These activities have nothing to do with the adaption of the VeriSM™ model. Adapting means that first principles, practices and an operating model need to be established.

B) Correct. These are the steps in adapting the VeriSM™ model. (Literature: A, Chapter 15.1)

C) Incorrect. VeriSM™ works with a Mesh, containing more practices. Adapting means that in addition to selecting practices, principles and an operating model need to be established.

D) Incorrect. VeriSM™ is not about selecting one practice, but about using the required practices together. Adapting means that principles, any new management practices and an operating model need to be established.

32

The Define stage of the VeriSM™ model produces a definition of what good service looks like.

During which process does this activity take place?

A) Create the service blueprint

B) Create the solution

C) Define consumer needs

D) Gather requirements

A) Incorrect. The service blueprint is the guiding document for the Produce stage. It contains a detailed specification of the service: the service level requirements, the support model as well as the measurements and reporting as agreed in the requirements gathering stage. (Literature: A, Chapter 11.6)

B) Incorrect. This is the process where the design is constructed including the method of measuring good performance for availability, capacity, continuity and security. (Literature: A, Chapter 11.5)

C) Incorrect. This is too early in the process. Consumer needs are often established in a business case, the approval of which then triggers further activities which result in performance measures being included in the service blueprint. (Literature: A, Chapter 11.3)

D) Correct. During the requirements gathering process the functional and non-functional requirements are established (including what good performance looks like). This drives the construction of the appropriate measures and reporting. (Literature: A, Chapter 11.4)

33

Which is the objective of service measurement?

A) To demonstrate compliance with laws, regulations and contractual commitments

B) To enable service providers to manage the performance capabilities of underpinning service elements

C) To enable the consumer to understand the costs of providing the service

D) To quantify and qualify the results or outcomes provided by a service

A) Incorrect. Compliance is one of the four service measurement considerations which helps enable management of the service. It is not the overall objective of measurement.

B) Incorrect. Whilst these measures are important for service providers, they are not of interest to consumers and do not reflect a holistic view of service measurement.

C) Incorrect. Understanding the cost of providing service is important to the service provider rather than the consumer. Consumers are more interested in the cost of consumption and the value they derive from the service.

D) Correct. Measuring a service begins by understanding the service and the consumer and how the consumer receives the value of the service. Measurement (and reporting) is the means by which value is demonstrated to the consumer. (Literature: A, Chapter 10.4.4.1)

34

An organization is growing rapidly and therefore wants to reconsider all their processes. They find that testing is too risky. They want to minimize costs of fixing errors resulting from late discovery of integration and test errors.

Which management practice would **best** address this issue?

A) Agile

B) CX/UX

C) Lean

D) SIAM

A) Incorrect. Agile includes the ability to think quickly, solve problems and have new ideas. An Agile organization would be fast moving, flexible and robust, capable of rapid responses to unexpected challenges, events and opportunities. Therefore Agile will not be the best management practice to address this issue.

B) Incorrect. CX/UX is the relationship between the consumers of products and services and the organization that produces them. This management practice will not address the costs associated with testing issues.

C) Correct. Both Lean and Continuous Delivery improve minimizing delays associated with testing efforts. They both also minimize testing risks and find integration and test errors before they become too expensive to fix. (Literature: A, Chapter 16.1)

D) Incorrect. SIAM focuses on defining a set of principles, practices and approaches used to manage, integrate, govern and coordinate the delivery of services from multiple service providers. SIAM does not specifically focus on minimizing costs associated with testing efforts.

35

How can Agile be used to support service management?

A) Agile cannot be used as it is a project management-only practice

B) For building products and services iteratively

C) For easy acceptance of all service management practices across the entire organization

D) To build all service management processes like traditional waterfall projects

A) Incorrect. Agile practices can be used not only in project management but also in business-as-usual activities and in service management.

B) Correct. Iteratively building products and services follows Agile techniques. (Literature: A, Chapter 17.5)

C) Incorrect. Agile promotes an iterative approach of introducing change step by step; gaining ongoing acceptance of service management practices in entire organization is continuous process.

D) Incorrect. Agile practices promote the iteratively building of service management processes. Waterfall is the traditional approach for the building service management process.

How does DevOps advance service management practices?

A) DevOps advances service management practices by shifting them to the left, making them leaner.

B) DevOps sets up the principles for service management practices.

C) DevOps should be used only to develop new products and services.

D) DevOps was established later than service management and therefore does not advance service management practices.

36

A) Correct. DevOps can advance service management practices by shifting them to the left, making them leaner and automating service management activities. (Literature: A, Chapter 18.7)

B) Incorrect. DevOps cannot set up principles as they are an inherent part of service management.

C) Incorrect. DevOps can be used to create new products and services as well as improving existing ones.

D) Incorrect. It does not matter DevOps was establish later because it can influence existing service management practices by involving people, development, operations, quality and testing.

31 / 40

What is the third layer between consumer and provider in Service and Integration Management (SIAM)?

A) Service advocate
B) Service installer
C) Service integrator
D) Service manager

A) Incorrect. There is no such role in SIAM, Best Management Practices and VeriSM™.

B) Incorrect. There is no such role in SIAM, Best Management Practices and VeriSM™.

C) Correct. This is the name of the third layer between consumer and provider in SIAM. (Literature: A, Chapter 19.2)

D) Incorrect. There is no such role in SIAM, Best Management Practices and VeriSM™.

37

In Lean, different types of waste are distinguished.

What type of waste is "producing at levels of quality more than required by the customer"?

A) Inventory

B) Overdelivering

C) Overprocessing

D) Overproduction

A) Incorrect. This type of waste is described as excess products and materials that are not being used.

B) Incorrect. This type of waste does not exist in Lean.

C) Correct. This is the description of overprocessing. (Literature: A, Chapter 20.7)

D) Incorrect. This type of waste is described as creating more output then is needed and before it is needed.

Shift Left is an approach which sees solution development, delivery and support pushed to earlier stages in their lifecycle and so gains efficiencies, cost savings and improved customer focus.

Which activity is **not** a feature of Shift Left?

A) Auto-correction of operational issues after they have occurred

B) Auto-detection of potential operational issues before they occur

C) Automatic incident referral to second line support

D) Self service incident diagnosis

38

A) Incorrect. This is a feature of Shift Left. Automatically resolving incidents reduces potential service downtime by negating the need for human intervention. For example, the effects of a power failure may be minimized by detection by event management and the automatic fail-over of service to alternative processing resources.

B) Incorrect. This is on the extreme left spectrum of Shift Left. Incidents are prevented and so support costs and service downtime are avoided. For example, event management may detect that a container is filling up and automatically triggers the addition of extra storage.

C) Correct. This is not a Shift Left activity because comparatively expensive second line resources are involved. Automation, however, is a key component of Shift Left as it reduces the risk of human error. Automated incident referral to second line support may well be, in certain circumstances, the most appropriate process - but it is not Shift Left. (Literature: A, Chapter 21)

D) Incorrect. Self-service is a Shift Left practice. It is "the backbone of level 0 support". Consumers can interrogate knowledge bases and use community forums and many other tools to find a resolution to their difficulty without having to contact comparatively expensive IT support. It is important, however, that IT support is aware of consumers' self-service activities so that they can moderate content.

34 / 40

What is the **first** step in building a customer journey map?

A) Define

B) Investigate

C) Plan

D) Research

A) Correct. This is the first step to build a customer journey map. (Literature: A, Chapter 22.7)

B) Incorrect. This is not a step in building a customer journey map.

C) Incorrect. This is a step in the Deming cycle but not in building a customer journey map.

D) Incorrect. This is the second step in building a customer journey map.

39

How does continuous delivery **positively** impact change control processes?

A) It does not impact the change control processes.

B) It impacts the processes through automated testing facilities.

C) It impacts the processes through delivering more information.

D) It impacts the processes through less rigorous change control.

A) Incorrect. Continuous delivery may positively impact change control processes by automation of the integration and testing process without human intervention or discussion.

B) Correct. Continuous delivery may impact change control process through the elimination of human intervention/human factor or discussion. (Literature: A, Chapter 23.7)

C) Incorrect. Adding more information means longer decision-making. This can negatively impact change control processes and not eliminate human errors.

D) Incorrect. A less rigorous change control process can impact more human failures and may negatively impact the whole process.

36 / 40

Technology is changing fast and this provides significant challenges for service management.

What is a generic challenge identified for service management?

A) Ensuring cost is matched to budget

B) Matching expectations to business relationships

C) More complexity and less visibility

D) Service management approaches support constraints

40

A) Incorrect. Ensuring cost is matched to budget is not one of the identified challenges for service management.

B) Incorrect. The challenge is to match expectations to reality, not to the relationships within the organization.

C) Correct. A recognized challenge is that emerging technologies and access to new technology can make the service provider's environment more complex. (Literature: A, Chapter 25.1)

D) Incorrect. Service management approaches need to support the organization, not the constraints.

37 / 40

What is a **key** benefit of cloud?

A) Enhanced internal communication

B) Increased quality of the infrastructure

C) Increased speed of infrastructure service

D) Reduced operating risks

41

A) Incorrect. Using cloud for the infrastructure will not have an impact on your ability to communicate internally. Using cloud may lead to benefits like reduced operating risks, quick provisioning of hardware and software resources, and increasing the ability to pay as you go.

B) Incorrect. Although putting infrastructure in the cloud may result in better quality, it is not a given. If there is a good internal infrastructure setup to begin with, you cannot expect an increase in quality merely by lifting it to the cloud. Using cloud may lead to benefits like reduced operating risks, quick provisioning of hardware and software resources, and increasing the ability to pay as you go.

C) Incorrect. Although you may experience higher speed of infrastructure service, this will only happen if your internal infrastructure was slow to begin with. If you have fast and efficient infrastructure service already, you cannot expect an improvement on this factor, merely by putting your infrastructure in the cloud. Using cloud may lead to benefits like reduced operating risks, quick provisioning of hardware and software resources, and increasing your ability to pay as you go.

D) Correct. The complexities of managing infrastructure servers, storage and applications is handled by the cloud provider allowing organizations to focus on core activities instead of IT technical tasks.
(Literature: A, Chapter 25.2)

38 / 40

An organization decides to use a SaaS solution to control their new Internet of Things (IoT) monitoring devices.

What is **most** important to consider from a service management point of view?

A) A key requirement is that IoT devices have unique identifiers and IP addresses.

B) IoT services provide better behavior tracking to support real-time marketing.

C) It is an outsourced service, so no specific considerations are required.

D) The guardrails for the services must be respected also for SaaS solutions.

42

Document version: v221217

A) Incorrect. This is a valid technical requirement, but not important form a service management view.

B) Incorrect. This is a benefit that IoT services provide, but not important form a service management view.

C) Incorrect. The service management principles apply for all services.

D) Correct. The guardrails are overall principles for all services, outsourced or not. (Literature: A, Chapter 1.4 and 25.6)

39 / 40

What is the advantage of Robotic Process Automation (RPA) in service management processes?

A) RPA automates tasks and therefore will always reduce headcount.

B) RPA helps in enabling employees to perform more complex tasks.

C) RPA increases the quality of the produced products as it automates tasks.

D) RPA is a manufacturing technique which cannot be used effectively in service management.

A) Incorrect. RPA is not always about reducing headcount.

B) Correct. Redeployment of staffing resources to more valuable activities is a clear benefit, and it has also automated more complex tasks involving advanced logic. (Literature: A, Chapter 25.8)

C) Incorrect. RPA in service management is not about product, but process task automation.

D) Incorrect. RPA is about automating (service management) process tasks.

43

An organization wants to break out of fire-fighting mode and move to the proactive mode.

On which element(s) of the VeriSM™ model should the focus be **first**?

A) Define and Produce

B) Governance

C) Management Mesh

D) Provide and Respond

A) Correct. Improving things from the start and producing better services is the way to go. The focus is on the Define and Produce activities, rather than repairing what went wrong. (Literature: A, Chapter 26.1)

B) Incorrect. Although these elements are important, they are not the first to focus on.

C) Incorrect. This is a necessary element for moving towards the VeriSM™ model, but does not help breaking out of the fire-fighting mode in the short term.

D) Incorrect. Focusing on what went wrong and trying to repair that, keeps the organization in fire-fight mode. The focus is on the Define and Produce activities, rather than repairing what went wrong.

44

VeriSM™ Essentials Sample Exam

1

Introduction

This is the sample exam VeriSM™ Essentials.

This exam consists of 20 multiple-choice questions. Each multiple-choice question has a number of possible answers, of which only one is the correct answer.

The maximum number of points that can be obtained for this exam is 20. Each correct answer is worth one point. If you obtain 13 points or more you will pass.

The time allowed for this exam is 30 minutes.

Good luck!

2

Sample exam

1 / 20
What is the **best** description of shadow behavior?

A) A junior observing a senior by doing job-shadowing and learning on-the-job
B) Creating a tribal system where team members are overshadowed by others
C) Implementing systems or solutions without explicit organizational approval
D) IT service provisioning being so good that consumers are unaware of IT

2 / 20
How does governance flow through an organization?

A) Via delegation from owners to a governing body, who authorize organizational capabilites to take actions to create and support the outcomes to consumers.
B) Via good planning in the higher levels of the organization, where it is critical that there is a clearly stated mission and vision with key objectives defined.
C) Via organization-wide gatherings once or twice a year, where owners/stakeholders present the mission, vision and objectives, and take feedback from employees.
D) Via performance contracts between an employee and his or her manager, making everybody responsible for part of the strategy.

3 / 20
New technology has led to changes within organizations.

Which is one of these changes?

A) Services are driven by stable management practices which discourage technology innovation.
B) Services can be delivered from anywhere to anywhere.
C) Services now undergo a more rigid functional change approach within organizations.
D) Services that rely on traditional rigid management approaches are preferable to organizations.

3

4 / 20

How can organizational culture **best** be described?

A) It is a collection of common practices based on the backgrounds of all employees within an organization.
B) It is a reflection of the ethnicity of management and owners within an organization.
C) It is a culture that is exclusively defined by the leadership of an organization.
D) It is a collection of, and interaction between, the values, systems, symbols, assumptions, beliefs and habits of an organization.

5 / 20

What is the **most** important element of creating a service culture?

A) Empowering the employees to make decisions on their own
B) Measuring the service culture in order to identify improvement ideas
C) Showing the consumer that they are valued by actions rather then telling them
D) Training employees and managers in good service behavior

6 / 20

Emotional intelligence defines two main competencies: personal and social.

Which two skills belong to the social competence?

A) Joining social groups and actively communicating with them
B) Knowing social media and what people or situations can influence us
C) Social awareness and relationship management
D) Social content management and using social techniques

7 / 20

What is the **last** stage of team formation?

A) Adjourning
B) Forming
C) Performing
D) Setting-up

4

8 / 20

There is a challenge that teams may operate in silos.

What is a recommendation that management should do to overcome this challenge?

A) Implement one-on-one meetings between team members
B) Provide team-building activities for each team
C) Reward teams who achieve their goals ahead of target
D) Share information on the organization's strategies

9 / 20

Successful expectation management depends on developing a clear vision of what is expected.

How can this clarity be achieved?

A) Ensure that detailed SLA documentation is available
B) Report achievement against agreed targets
C) Set boundaries and provide a structure for delivery
D) Under-promise and over-deliver

10 / 20

What is one of the five components that should be considered in communication?

A) Delivery mechanism
B) Intention
C) Perception
D) Scope

11 / 20

Which element of the VeriSM™ model defines the management activities or practices necessary to meet the governance requirements by providing guardrails or boundaries?

A) Define
B) Management Mesh
C) Produce
D) Service management principles

5

12 / 20

Following the deployment of a new product or service, the service provider will provide ongoing support in its use to consumers.

Which element of the VeriSM™ model describes this provision of support?

A) Define
B) Produce
C) Provide
D) Respond

13 / 20

What is the **main** reason VeriSM™ re-defines traditional service management?

A) VeriSM™ divides service management within an organization into separate entities so all entities can work autonomously.
B) VeriSM™ focuses on the big picture and does not provide practices for specific organizations.
C) VeriSM™ incorporates new technologies and therefore helps IT departments with digital transformation.
D) VeriSM™ regards the entire organization as the service provider with capabilities that work together.

14 / 20

What differentiates VeriSM™ from other IT service management approaches?

A) VeriSM™ differentiates IT from other service management practices.
B) VeriSM™ focuses on the corporate IT aspects in the organization.
C) VeriSM™ is a logical evolution to older IT service management practices.
D) VeriSM™ takes all organizational capabilities into account.

15 / 20

VeriSM™ introduces the concept of the Management Mesh. This combines the four elements of resources, management practices, environment and emerging technologies to create and deliver products and services.

In which element should frameworks such as ITIL or methodologies such as COBIT be included?

A) Emerging technologies
B) Environment
C) Management practices
D) Resources

6

The Management Mesh can only be built once the organizational governance and service management principles are understood.

What else must also be developed before the Mesh is built?

A) Design specifications
B) Operational plans
C) Strategic plans
D) Tactical plans

What is an objective of the Define stage in the VeriSM™ model?

A) To address activities and supporting outcomes that relate to the design of a product or service
B) To ensure the product or service is available for consumption
C) To react to service issues, inquiries and requests from the consumer
D) To take the service blueprint and perform build, test and implement activities under change control

Why is testing an important part of the Produce stage?

A) To define risk criteria and the risk appetite of an organization
B) To ensure that the product or service meets the requirements set
C) To ensure that the organization's requirements are in line with its strategy
D) To ensure an organization's architecture is appropriate

What activity is part of the Provide stage?

A) Build
B) Design
C) Improve
D) Test

What is covered by the activity Record in the Respond stage?

A) Capture information
B) Deliver results
C) Resolve the issue
D) Source events

7

8

Answer key

1 / 20

What is the **best** description of shadow behavior?

A) A junior observing a senior by doing job-shadowing and learning on-the-job

B) Creating a tribal system where team members are overshadowed by others

C) Implementing systems or solutions without explicit organizational approval

D) IT service provisioning being so good that consumers are unaware of IT

A) Incorrect. Although job-shadowing is a valid skills development approach which yields good results, it has no bearing on shadow behavior. Shadow behavior is about things such as the introduction of systems into the live environment without approval.

B) Incorrect. VeriSM™ removes the barriers and tribalism found in many organizations. Overshadowing other team members is considered undesirable behavior and should be avoided according to VeriSM ™, but shadow behavior focusses on the lack of explicit organizational approval for changes in organizations.

C) Correct. Shadow behavior and specifically shadow IT is a big problem in organizations. Not following organizational approval processes and procedures (change management) introduces unknown risks into the environment and may well have an impact on the performance of other IT services. (Literature: A, Chapter 2.3.1)

D) Incorrect. It is a good thing if IT services are seen as non-intrusive and if services forms part of the functioning of the organization. However shadow behavior is not positive as it means things such as systems being implemented without approval and thereby increasing risk.

9

How does governance flow through an organization?

A) Via delegation from owners to a governing body, who authorize organizational capabilites to take actions to create and support the outcomes to consumers.

B) Via good planning in the higher levels of the organization, where it is critical that there is a clearly stated mission and vision with key objectives defined.

C) Via organization-wide gatherings once or twice a year, where owners/stakeholders present the mission, vision and objectives, and take feedback from employees.

D) Via performance contracts between an employee and his or her manager, making everybody responsible for part of the strategy.

A) Correct. There needs to be an actual frame of delegation and authorization supporting the flow of governance for it to really work. (Literature: A, Chapter 2.5.2)

B) Incorrect. Although strategic planning in the higher levels of the organization is important, it cannot be considered the backbone of how the governance flows. It will flow via delegation to a governing body, who will authorize the organizational capabilites to take action based on the mission, vision and objectives.

C) Incorrect. Although openness and invitation to dialogue from owners/stakeholders about the mission, vision and objectives may be advised, it cannot be considered the backbone of how the governance flows. It will flow via delegation to a governing body, who will authorize the organizational capabilites to take action based on the mission, vision and objectives.

D) Incorrect. Although having commitments between a manager and an employee is a good idea to ensure that everybody understands, and is accountable for their contribution to the mission, vision and objectives of the organization, there needs to be an equally strong commitment and accountability between the owners/stakeholders, who make the mission, vision and objectives, and a governing body. Who then in turn authorizes for instance managers to bring the mission, vision and objectives to life.

10

New technology has led to changes within organizations.

Which is one of these changes?

A) Services are driven by stable management practices which discourage technology innovation.

B) Services can be delivered from anywhere to anywhere.

C) Services now undergo a more rigid functional change approach within organizations.

D) Services that rely on traditional rigid management approaches are preferable to organizations.

A) Incorrect. Although stability is still important, the speed of technology change requires greater innovation, not less.

B) Correct. New innovative technologies have allowed services to be delivered from anywhere, to anywhere. (Literature: A, Chapter 3.1)

C) Incorrect. Agile approaches provide the desired flexibility, rather than rigid management.

D) Incorrect. Organizations are looking for more Agile and flexible approaches to service management, to cater for a fast changing environment.

4 / 20

How can organizational culture **best** be described?

A) It is a collection of common practices based on the backgrounds of all employees within an organization.

B) It is a reflection of the ethnicity of management and owners within an organization.

C) It is a culture that is exclusively defined by the leadership of an organization.

D) It is a collection of, and interaction between, the values, systems, symbols, assumptions, beliefs and habits of an organization.

11

A) Incorrect. VeriSM™ defines organizational culture as "the collection of written and unwritten rules, guidelines and practices that shape the behaviors of the people in an organization". The answer may seem correct but to say that common practices based on employee backgrounds is not correct. Employees certainly influence organizational culture but it is only one of many factors that influence culture.

B) Incorrect. Although the context in which an organization operates and managers' and owners' backgrounds influence organizational culture, a number of other factors do too. Cultural references from one group of organizational stakeholders should not form the exclusive basis of organizational culture.

C) Incorrect. The leadership of an organization certainly has a major influence on and may actively affect organizational culture, but it is by no means the only determining factor. Leaders and managers that attempt organizational change that opposes organizational culture will soon find out that this is a difficult and sometimes dangerous task and they will mostly see their change initiatives fail.

D) Correct. Culture is 'the way we do things in an organization'. According to VeriSM™ a good description would be "the collective values, systems, symbols, assumptions, beliefs and habits of an organization". All of these can be observed in how things are done in the organization. Culture is often not formally defined, written down or taught to new employees. They will mostly "observe and learn how things are done here". (Literature: A, Chapter 2.4)

5 / 20

What is the **most** important element of creating a service culture?

A) Empowering the employees to make decisions on their own

B) Measuring the service culture in order to identify improvement ideas

C) Showing the consumer that they are valued by actions rather then telling them

D) Training employees and managers in good service behavior

12

A) Incorrect. Although empowerment is one of the areas senior management needs to focus on in order to bring about a service culture, it is not the most important element of a service culture. Actually showing the consumer that they are valued by actions rather than just telling them they are valued, is the most important element though.

B) Incorrect. In order to know whether you are doing a good job, it is important to measure your performance. However, it is not the most critical element in bringing about a service culture as such. Actually showing the consumer that they are valued by actions rather than just telling them they are valued, is the most important element though.

C) Correct. Making the consumer feel that they are valued is the most important element of a service culture. (Literature: A, Chapter 4.4)

D) Incorrect. In order to bring about a service culture in an organization, it is important that employees and management are actually enabled to do so, and to spot good behavior when they see it (or when they do not). Actually showing the consumer that they are valued by actions rather than just telling them they are valued, is the most important element of creating a service culture though.

6 / 20

Emotional intelligence defines two main competencies: personal and social.

Which two skills belong to the social competence?

A) Joining social groups and actively communicating with them
B) Knowing social media and what people or situations can influence us
C) Social awareness and relationship management
D) Social content management and using social techniques

13

A) Incorrect. Joining social groups and communication between group members are activities not skills.

B) Incorrect. Knowing social media is not enough to express it as a skill. Knowing what people and situations can influence ourselves is a skill that belongs to the personal competence.

C) Correct. Social awareness and relationship management are two skills defined by Travis Bradberry and Jean Greaves in their work "Emotional Intelligence 2.0". (Literature: A, Chapter 5.3)

D) Incorrect. Social content management and using social techniques are not skills. Techniques are the use of specific tools, a set of rules of conduct, and skills are immanent, acquired during the learning process and growth. Techniques are how to do something, skills are how to know and understand something.

7 / 20

What is the **last** stage of team formation?

A) Adjourning

B) Forming

C) Performing

D) Setting-up

A) Correct. This is the last stage in the formation of a team. It is when group tasks are complete and the team disbands. The other four stages are forming, storming, norming, and performing. (Literature: A, Chapter 5.7.1)

B) Incorrect. This is the first stage in a team formation. It focuses on getting to know each other and understand the purpose of the team.

C) Incorrect. This is the fourth stage in the formation of a team. During this stage relationships, team practices and effectiveness are synced and the real work of the team is now progressing.

D) Incorrect. This is not a stage in a team formation.

14

There is a challenge that teams may operate in silos.

What is a recommendation that management should do to overcome this challenge?

A) Implement one-on-one meetings between team members

B) Provide team-building activities for each team

C) Reward teams who achieve their goals ahead of target

D) Share information on the organization's strategies

A) Incorrect. Such meetings are helpful in building a team spirit across a virtual team, but may encourage the development of silos, by encouraging the team to look inwards.

B) Incorrect. Team building activities for each team will encourage team spirit, but not collaboration with other teams.

C) Incorrect. Rewarding teams for achieving goals ahead of target may emphasize competition and discourage collaboration with other teams.

D) Correct. Sharing the organization's strategic aims will help to focus the teams on the bigger picture, so that the team works to help to achieve the overall objective. (Literature: A, Chapter 6.1)

Successful expectation management depends on developing a clear vision of what is expected.

How can this clarity be achieved?

A) Ensure that detailed SLA documentation is available

B) Report achievement against agreed targets

C) Set boundaries and provide a structure for delivery

D) Under-promise and over-deliver

15

A) Incorrect. Detailed documentation may not necessarily improve clarity, if it is overly complex or ambiguous. Service level agreements must be clear and state the level of service to be provided and how this is to be measured.

B) Incorrect. There is a danger that targets may be met, but the overall perception of the end-to-end service is poor, if the targets are not aligned to the business requirement. This is known as the watermelon effect (green on the outside, red on the inside).

C) Correct. Defining the scope of what is to be delivered in an unambiguous way will ensure that all parties are in agreement and prevent a mismatch between expectations and delivery. (Literature: A, Chapter 6.2.1)

D) Incorrect. The ambition to under-promise and then deliver a better service than agreed does not help clarify expectations, and may even raise expectations to an achievable level over time, as there is no clear agreement on what the service provider is able to provide.

What is one of the five components that should be considered in communication?

A) Delivery mechanism

B) Intention

C) Perception

D) Scope

16

A) Correct. In good communication there are five components to consider. These five components are: sender, context, receiver, delivery mechanism and content. (Literature: A, Chapter 6.4)

B) Incorrect. Intention is not one of the five components to consider in communication. Every message should have a defined purpose (intent) that the sender wants to achieve with the communication.

C) Incorrect. Perception is not one of the five components to consider in communication. It is how the message is understood.

D) Incorrect. Scope is not one of the five components to consider in communication. The scope is a part of a defined communication plan.

11 / 20

Which element of the VeriSM™ model defines the management activities or practices necessary to meet the governance requirements by providing guardrails or boundaries?

A) Define

B) Management Mesh

C) Produce

D) Service management principles

17

A) Incorrect. The Define stage is concerned with the activities and supporting outcomes that relate to the design of a product or service. The Define stage works within the guardrails provided by the service management principles.

B) Incorrect. The Management Mesh does not provide the guardrails; it allows teams to work on products and services flexibly, combining resources, practices, environment and emerging technologies.

C) Incorrect. The Produce stage is concerned with the creation of the solution, ensuring the outcome meets the needs of the consumer. The Produce stage works within the guardrails provided by the service management principles.

D) Correct. The service management principles are based on the organizational governing principles. They provide the guardrails for the products and services delivered, addressing areas such as quality and risk. (Literature: A, Chapter 7 and Chapter 9.1)

12 / 20

Following the deployment of a new product or service, the service provider will provide ongoing support in its use to consumers.

Which element of the VeriSM™ model describes this provision of support?

A) Define

B) Produce

C) Provide

D) Respond

18

A) Incorrect. The Define stage is concerned with the activities and supporting outcomes that relate to the design of a product or service.

B) Incorrect. The Produce stage is concerned with the creation of the solution, ensuring the outcome meets the needs of the consumer.

C) Incorrect. The Provide stage is concerned with making the new or changed solution available for use.

D) Correct. The Respond stage describes the support the consumer receives during performance issues, questions or any other requests. (Literature: A, Chapter 7 and 14.1)

13 / 20

What is the **main** reason VeriSM™ re-defines traditional service management?

A) VeriSM™ divides service management within an organization into separate entities so all entities can work autonomously.

B) VeriSM™ focuses on the big picture and does not provide practices for specific organizations.

C) VeriSM™ incorporates new technologies and therefore helps IT departments with digital transformation.

D) VeriSM™ regards the entire organization as the service provider with capabilities that work together.

A) Incorrect. VeriSM™ has a holistic view for the whole organization and it does not separate an organization into entities.

B) Incorrect. VeriSM™ provides a Mesh to personalize service management for a specific organization.

C) Incorrect. This is true, but not the main reason why it re-defines service management.

D) Correct. This is the key differentiator between VeriSM™ and ITSM. (Literature: A, Chapter 9.2)

19

What differentiates VeriSM™ from other IT service management approaches?

A) VeriSM™ differentiates IT from other service management practices.

B) VeriSM™ focuses on the corporate IT aspects in the organization.

C) VeriSM™ is a logical evolution to older IT service management practices.

D) VeriSM™ takes all organizational capabilities into account.

A) Incorrect. VeriSM™ regards all departments and area's as capabilities in delivering consumer services.

B) Incorrect. VeriSM™ focuses on the whole organization, not just IT.

C) Incorrect. VeriSM™ is the next step, but has a broader focus then traditional IT service management.

D) Correct. VeriSM™ has a holistic view over the organization as a whole. The entire organization is the service provider and the individual departments are the capabilities that support the organization as it delivers products and services. (Literature: A, Chapter 9.2)

VeriSM™ introduces the concept of the Management Mesh. This combines the four elements of resources, management practices, environment and emerging technologies to create and deliver products and services.

In which element should frameworks such as ITIL or methodologies such as COBIT be included?

A) Emerging technologies

B) Environment

C) Management practices

D) Resources

20

A) Incorrect. Emerging technologies are the advances in overall technologies such as cloud services, automation and the Internet of Things which may be exploited when designing and delivering a service.

B) Incorrect. The environmental aspects include the organizational culture, market position, and regulatory framework.

C) Correct. The management practices element of the Mesh includes frameworks such as ITIL, and methodologies such as COBIT, SIAM and DevOps. The organization chooses which to use, dependent on the requirement. (Literature: A: Chapter 10)

D) Incorrect. Resources are the elements an organization draws on to create products and services, such as people, money and assets.

16 / 20

The Management Mesh can only be built once the organizational governance and service management principles are understood.

What else must also be developed before the Mesh is built?

A) Design specifications

B) Operational plans

C) Strategic plans

D) Tactical plans

A) Incorrect. The Management Mesh is used to develop and deliver products and services. The design specifications are developed using the Management Mesh.

B) Incorrect. Operational plans are developed following the building of the Management Mesh. Based on the requirements, the service provider chooses the best elements for the Mesh to create the operational plan.

C) Correct. Working within the guardrails set by the organizational governance and service management principles, the service provider develops their strategic plans to address consumer requirements. Based on these, the Management Mesh is built. (Literature: A, Chapter 10.5)

D) Incorrect. Tactical plans are developed following the building of the Management Mesh. Based on the requirements, the service provider chooses the best elements for the Mesh to create the tactical plan.

17 / 20

What is an objective of the Define stage in the VeriSM™ model?

A) To address activities and supporting outcomes that relate to the design of a product or service

B) To ensure the product or service is available for consumption

C) To react to service issues, inquiries and requests from the consumer

D) To take the service blueprint and perform build, test and implement activities under change control

A) Correct. Define is about addressing the activities relating to the design of a service or product. (Literature: A, Chapter 11.1)

B) Incorrect. This is an objective for the Provide stage of the VeriSM™ model.

C) Incorrect. This is an objective for the Respond stage of the VeriSM™ model.

D) Incorrect. This is an objective for the Produce stage of the VeriSM™ model.

22

Why is testing an important part of the Produce stage?

A) To define risk criteria and the risk appetite of an organization

B) To ensure that the product or service meets the requirements set

C) To ensure that the organization's requirements are in line with its strategy

D) To ensure an organization's architecture is appropriate

A) Incorrect. The organizational appetite for risk is the responsibility of governance structures and risk criteria associated to a product of service are defined during the Define stage. Testing needs to make sure that the introduction of a new or changed service or product meets the requirements set with regards to risk and not to define what these requirements are.

B) Correct. Testing needs to ensure that the product or service meets the requirements set in the Design stage. This may include a number of tests that checks, for instance, if the product or service will meet the stakeholder needs that prompted the development of the product or service. Checking whether a service or product meets requirements set in the Define stage normally include activities like testing functionality, usability, technical compatibility etcetera, but testing should also ensure that the product or service enables business outcomes and facilitate the realization of business value. (Literature: A, Chapter 7 and Chapter 12.5)

C) Incorrect. Validating whether organizational requirements support the organization's strategy is the responsibility of the governing body and management and not the objective of testing. However, the VeriSM™ model may provide valuable feedback to management and governance structures to that end.

D) Incorrect. Evaluating the appropriateness of organizational architecture is a management activity. Testing should ensure that products and services are aligned with the defined organizational architecture and not the other way around.

23

What activity is part of the Provide stage?

A) Build

B) Design

C) Improve

D) Test

A) Incorrect. Build is a part of the Produce stage of the VeriSM™ Model. Build turns the service blueprint produced in the Define stage into actionable plans and then into action that produce the new or changed service.

B) Incorrect. It is not a part of the Provide stage. Design is not an activity of the Define stage of the VeriSM™ model but could rather be seen as a partial description of what is done in the Define stage, especially during requirements outcome, solution and the service blueprint activities.

C) Correct. Improve is an activity of the Provide stage of the VeriSM™ model. Improve includes maintenance and improvement activities. (Literature: A, Chapter 13.2)

D) Incorrect. Test is part of the Produce stage and ensures that the product or service is tested according to the designed plans. These tests should cover a variety of circumstances and will be based on organizational governance.

What is covered by the activity Record in the Respond stage?

A) Capture information

B) Deliver results

C) Resolve the issue

D) Source events

24

A) Correct. Capturing information is covered by the Record activity. (Literature: A, Chapter 14.2)

B) Incorrect. Delivering results is covered by the Manage activity.

C) Incorrect. Resolving issues is covered by the Manage activity.

D) Incorrect. Sourcing events is covered by the Manage activity.

25

VeriSM™ Plus Sample Exam

1

Introduction

This is the sample exam VeriSM™ Plus.

This exam consists of 20 multiple-choice questions. Each multiple-choice question has a number of possible answers, of which only one is the correct answer.

The maximum number of points that can be obtained for this exam is 20. Each correct answer is worth one point. If you obtain 13 points or more you will pass.

The time allowed for this exam is 30 minutes.

Good luck!

2

Sample exam

1 / 20
New technology has led to changes within organizations.

Which is one of these changes?

A) Services are driven by stable management practices which discourage technology innovation.
B) Services can be delivered from anywhere to anywhere.
C) Services now undergo a more rigid functional change approach within organizations.
D) Services that rely on traditional rigid management approaches are preferable to organizations.

2 / 20
What is the key activity of a leader's role?

A) Focus on results
B) Minimize risk
C) Motivate colleagues
D) Set up priorities

3 / 20
Emotional intelligence defines two main competencies: personal and social.

Which two skills belong to the social competence?

A) Joining social groups and actively communicating with them
B) Knowing social media and what people or situations can influence us
C) Social awareness and relationship management
D) Social content management and using social techniques

4 / 20
What is the **last** stage of team formation?

A) Adjourning
B) Forming
C) Performing
D) Setting-up

3

5 / 20
What is the **main** reason VeriSM™ re-defines traditional service management?

A) VeriSM™ divides service management within an organization into separate entities so all entities can work autonomously.
B) VeriSM™ focuses on the big picture and does not provide practices for specific organizations.
C) VeriSM™ incorporates new technologies and therefore helps IT departments with digital transformation.
D) VeriSM™ regards the entire organization as the service provider with capabilities that work together.

6 / 20
Why is testing an important part of the Produce stage?

A) To define risk criteria and the risk appetite of an organization
B) To ensure that the product or service meets the requirements set
C) To ensure that the organization's requirements are in line with its strategy
D) To ensure an organization's architecture is appropriate

7 / 20
What activity is part of the Provide stage?

A) Build
B) Design
C) Improve
D) Test

8 / 20
What steps describe the high-level process for adapting the VeriSM™ model?

A) Define the stakeholders, select the processes, and implement them in the organization
B) Establish the principles, select a set of practices, create a responsive operating model
C) Investigate all practices in use, select the best set, and make these mandatory
D) Select the best management practice, focus thereon, and implement it step by step

4

9 / 20

The Define stage of the VeriSM™ model produces a definition of what good service looks like.

During which process does this activity take place?

A) Create the service blueprint
B) Create the solution
C) Define consumer needs
D) Gather requirements

10 / 20

Which is the objective of service measurement?

A) To demonstrate compliance with laws, regulations and contractual commitments
B) To enable service providers to manage the performance capabilities of underpinning service elements
C) To enable the consumer to understand the costs of providing the service
D) To quantify and qualify the results or outcomes provided by a service

11 / 20

An organization is growing rapidly and therefore wants to reconsider all their processes. They find that testing is too risky. They want to minimize costs of fixing errors resulting from late discovery of integration and test errors.

Which management practice would **best** address this issue?

A) Agile
B) CX/UX
C) Lean
D) SIAM

12 / 20

How can Agile be used to support service management?

A) Agile cannot be used as it is a project management-only practice
B) For building products and services iteratively
C) For easy acceptance of all service management practices across the entire organization
D) To build all service management processes like traditional waterfall projects

5

13 / 20
How does DevOps advance service management practices?

A) DevOps advances service management practices by shifting them to the left, making them leaner.
B) DevOps sets up the principles for service management practices.
C) DevOps should be used only to develop new products and services.
D) DevOps was established later than service management and therefore does not advance service management practices.

14 / 20
In Lean, different types of waste are distinguished.

What type of waste is "producing at levels of quality more than required by the customer"?

A) Inventory
B) Overdelivering
C) Overprocessing
D) Overproduction

15 / 20
What is the **first** step in building a customer journey map?

A) Define
B) Investigate
C) Plan
D) Research

16 / 20
How does continuous delivery **positively** impact change control processes?

A) It does not impact the change control processes.
B) It impacts the processes through automated testing facilities.
C) It impacts the processes through delivering more information.
D) It impacts the processes through less rigorous change control.

6

17 / 20

Technology is changing fast and this provides significant challenges for service management.

What is a generic challenge identified for service management?

A) Ensuring cost is matched to budget
B) Matching expectations to business relationships
C) More complexity and less visibility
D) Service management approaches support constraints

18 / 20

What is a **key** benefit of cloud?

A) Enhanced internal communication
B) Increased quality of the infrastructure
C) Increased speed of infrastructure service
D) Reduced operating risks

19 / 20

An organization decides to use a SaaS solution to control their new Internet of Things (IoT) monitoring devices.

What is **most** important to consider from a service management point of view?

A) A key requirement is that IoT devices have unique identifiers and IP addresses.
B) IoT services provide better behavior tracking to support real-time marketing.
C) It is an outsourced service, so no specific considerations are required.
D) The guardrails for the services must be respected also for SaaS solutions.

20 / 20

An organization wants to break out of fire-fighting mode and move to the proactive mode.

On which element(s) of the VeriSM™ model should the focus be **first**?

A) Define and Produce
B) Governance
C) Management Mesh
D) Provide and Respond

7

Answer key

1 / 20

New technology has led to changes within organizations.

Which is one of these changes?

A) Services are driven by stable management practices which discourage technology innovation.

B) Services can be delivered from anywhere to anywhere.

C) Services now undergo a more rigid functional change approach within organizations.

D) Services that rely on traditional rigid management approaches are preferable to organizations.

A) Incorrect. Although stability is still important, the speed of technology change requires greater innovation, not less.

B) Correct. New innovative technologies have allowed services to be delivered from anywhere, to anywhere. (Literature: A, Chapter 3.1)

C) Incorrect. Agile approaches provide the desired flexibility, rather than rigid management.

D) Incorrect. Organizations are looking for more Agile and flexible approaches to service management, to cater for a fast changing environment.

2 / 20

What is the key activity of a leader's role?

A) Focus on results

B) Minimize risk

C) Motivate colleagues

D) Set up priorities

8

A) Incorrect. This is a key activity of the role of a manager.

B) Incorrect. This is a key activity of the role of a manager.

C) Correct. This activity is a key characteristic that is connected with the role of a leader in VeriSM™. Other key characteristics are empower and inspire. (Literature: A, Chapter 5.1)

D) Incorrect. This is a key activity of a Product Owner in a Scrum project.

3 / 20

Emotional intelligence defines two main competencies: personal and social.

Which two skills belong to the social competence?

A) Joining social groups and actively communicating with them

B) Knowing social media and what people or situations can influence us

C) Social awareness and relationship management

D) Social content management and using social techniques

A) Incorrect. Joining social groups and communication between group members are activities not skills.

B) Incorrect. Knowing social media is not enough to express it as a skill. Knowing what people and situations can influence ourselves is a skill that belongs to the personal competence.

C) Correct. Social awareness and relationship management are two skills defined by Travis Bradberry and Jean Greaves in their work "Emotional Intelligence 2.0". (Literature: A, Chapter 5.3)

D) Incorrect. Social content management and using social techniques are not skills. Techniques are the use of specific tools, a set of rules of conduct, and skills are immanent, acquired during the learning process and growth. Techniques are how to do something, skills are how to know and understand something.

9

What is the **last** stage of team formation?

A) Adjourning

B) Forming

C) Performing

D) Setting-up

A) Correct. This is the last stage in the formation of a team. It is when group tasks are complete and the team disbands. The other four stages are forming, storming, norming, and performing. (Literature: A, Chapter 5.7.1)

B) Incorrect. This is the first stage in a team formation. It focuses on getting to know each other and understand the purpose of the team.

C) Incorrect. This is the fourth stage in the formation of a team. During this stage relationships, team practices and effectiveness are synced and the real work of the team is now progressing.

D) Incorrect. This is not a stage in a team formation.

5 / 20

What is the **main** reason VeriSM™ re-defines traditional service management?

A) VeriSM™ divides service management within an organization into separate entities so all entities can work autonomously.

B) VeriSM™ focuses on the big picture and does not provide practices for specific organizations.

C) VeriSM™ incorporates new technologies and therefore helps IT departments with digital transformation.

D) VeriSM™ regards the entire organization as the service provider with capabilities that work together.

10

A) Incorrect. VeriSM™ has a holistic view for the whole organization and it does not separate an organization into entities.

B) Incorrect. VeriSM™ provides a Mesh to personalize service management for a specific organization.

C) Incorrect. This is true, but not the main reason why it re-defines service management.

D) Correct. This is the key differentiator between VeriSM™ and ITSM. (Literature: A, Chapter 9.2)

6 / 20

Why is testing an important part of the Produce stage?

A) To define risk criteria and the risk appetite of an organization

B) To ensure that the product or service meets the requirements set

C) To ensure that the organization's requirements are in line with its strategy

D) To ensure an organization's architecture is appropriate

11

A) Incorrect. The organizational appetite for risk is the responsibility of governance structures and risk criteria associated to a product of service are defined during the Define stage. Testing needs to make sure that the introduction of a new or changed service or product meets the requirements set with regards to risk and not to define what these requirements are.

B) Correct. Testing needs to ensure that the product or service meets the requirements set in the Design stage. This may include a number of tests that checks, for instance, if the product or service will meet the stakeholder needs that prompted the development of the product or service. Checking whether a service or product meets requirements set in the Define stage normally include activities like testing functionality, usability, technical compatibility etcetera, but testing should also ensure that the product or service enables business outcomes and facilitate the realization of business value. (Literature: A, Chapter 7 and Chapter 12.5)

C) Incorrect. Validating whether organizational requirements support the organization's strategy is the responsibility of the governing body and management and not the objective of testing. However, the VeriSM™ model may provide valuable feedback to management and governance structures to that end.

D) Incorrect. Evaluating the appropriateness of organizational architecture is a management activity. Testing should ensure that products and services are aligned with the defined organizational architecture and not the other way around.

7 / 20

What activity is part of the Provide stage?

A) Build

B) Design

C) Improve

D) Test

12

A) Incorrect. Build is a part of the Produce stage of the VeriSM™ Model. Build turns the service blueprint produced in the Define stage into actionable plans and then into action that produce the new or changed service.

B) Incorrect. It is not a part of the Provide stage. Design is not an activity of the Define stage of the VeriSM™ model but could rather be seen as a partial description of what is done in the Define stage, especially during requirements outcome, solution and the service blueprint activities.

C) Correct. Improve is an activity of the Provide stage of the VeriSM™ model. Improve includes maintenance and improvement activities. (Literature: A, Chapter 13.2)

D) Incorrect. Test is part of the Produce stage and ensures that the product or service is tested according to the designed plans. These tests should cover a variety of circumstances and will be based on organizational governance.

8 / 20

What steps describe the high-level process for adapting the VeriSM™ model?

A) Define the stakeholders, select the processes, and implement them in the organization

B) Establish the principles, select a set of practices, create a responsive operating model

C) Investigate all practices in use, select the best set, and make these mandatory

D) Select the best management practice, focus thereon, and implement it step by step

A) Incorrect. These activities have nothing to do with the adaption of the VeriSM™ model. Adapting means that first principles, practices and an operating model need to be established.

B) Correct. These are the steps in adapting the VeriSM™ model. (Literature: A, Chapter 15.1)

C) Incorrect. VeriSM™ works with a Mesh, containing more practices. Adapting means that in addition to selecting practices, principles and an operating model need to be established.

D) Incorrect. VeriSM™ is not about selecting one practice, but about using the required practices together. Adapting means that principles, any new management practices and an operating model need to be established.

13

The Define stage of the VeriSM™ model produces a definition of what good service looks like.

During which process does this activity take place?

A) Create the service blueprint

B) Create the solution

C) Define consumer needs

D) Gather requirements

A) Incorrect. The service blueprint is the guiding document for the Produce stage. It contains a detailed specification of the service: the service level requirements, the support model as well as the measurements and reporting as agreed in the requirements gathering stage. (Literature: A, Chapter 11.6)

B) Incorrect. This is the process where the design is constructed including the method of measuring good performance for availability, capacity, continuity and security. (Literature: A, Chapter 11.5)

C) Incorrect. This is too early in the process. Consumer needs are often established in a business case, the approval of which then triggers further activities which result in performance measures being included in the service blueprint. (Literature: A, Chapter 11.3)

D) Correct. During the requirements gathering process the functional and non-functional requirements are established (including what good performance looks like). This drives the construction of the appropriate measures and reporting. (Literature: A, Chapter 11.4)

14

Which is the objective of service measurement?

A) To demonstrate compliance with laws, regulations and contractual commitments

B) To enable service providers to manage the performance capabilities of underpinning service elements

C) To enable the consumer to understand the costs of providing the service

D) To quantify and qualify the results or outcomes provided by a service

A) Incorrect. Compliance is one of the four service measurement considerations which helps enable management of the service. It is not the overall objective of measurement.

B) Incorrect. Whilst these measures are important for service providers, they are not of interest to consumers and do not reflect a holistic view of service measurement.

C) Incorrect. Understanding the cost of providing service is important to the service provider rather than the consumer. Consumers are more interested in the cost of consumption and the value they derive from the service.

D) Correct. Measuring a service begins by understanding the service and the consumer and how the consumer receives the value of the service. Measurement (and reporting) is the means by which value is demonstrated to the consumer. (Literature: A, Chapter 10.4.4.1)

15

Document version: v221217

An organization is growing rapidly and therefore wants to reconsider all their processes. They find that testing is too risky. They want to minimize costs of fixing errors resulting from late discovery of integration and test errors.

Which management practice would **best** address this issue?

A) Agile

B) CX/UX

C) Lean

D) SIAM

A) Incorrect. Agile includes the ability to think quickly, solve problems and have new ideas. An Agile organization would be fast moving, flexible and robust, capable of rapid responses to unexpected challenges, events and opportunities. Therefore Agile will not be the best management practice to address this issue.

B) Incorrect. CX/UX is the relationship between the consumers of products and services and the organization that produces them. This management practice will not address the costs associated with testing issues.

C) Correct. Both Lean and Continuous Delivery improve minimizing delays associated with testing efforts. They both also minimize testing risks and find integration and test errors before they become too expensive to fix. (Literature: A, Chapter 16.1)

D) Incorrect. SIAM focuses on defining a set of principles, practices and approaches used to manage, integrate, govern and coordinate the delivery of services from multiple service providers. SIAM does not specifically focus on minimizing costs associated with testing efforts.

16

Document version: v221217

How can Agile be used to support service management?

A) Agile cannot be used as it is a project management-only practice

B) For building products and services iteratively

C) For easy acceptance of all service management practices across the entire organization

D) To build all service management processes like traditional waterfall projects

A) Incorrect. Agile practices can be used not only in project management but also in business-as-usual activities and in service management.

B) Correct. Iteratively building products and services follows Agile techniques. (Literature: A, Chapter 17.5)

C) Incorrect. Agile promotes an iterative approach of introducing change step by step; gaining ongoing acceptance of service management practices in entire organization is continuous process.

D) Incorrect. Agile practices promote the iteratively building of service management processes. Waterfall is the traditional approach for the building service management process.

13 / 20

How does DevOps advance service management practices?

A) DevOps advances service management practices by shifting them to the left, making them leaner.

B) DevOps sets up the principles for service management practices.

C) DevOps should be used only to develop new products and services.

D) DevOps was established later than service management and therefore does not advance service management practices.

17

Document version: v221217

A) Correct. DevOps can advance service management practices by shifting them to the left, making them leaner and automating service management activities. (Literature: A, Chapter 18.7)

B) Incorrect. DevOps cannot set up principles as they are an inherent part of service management.

C) Incorrect. DevOps can be used to create new products and services as well as improving existing ones.

D) Incorrect. It does not matter DevOps was establish later because it can influence existing service management practices by involving people, development, operations, quality and testing.

14 / 20

In Lean, different types of waste are distinguished.

What type of waste is "producing at levels of quality more than required by the customer"?

A) Inventory
B) Overdelivering
C) Overprocessing
D) Overproduction

A) Incorrect. This type of waste is described as excess products and materials that are not being used.

B) Incorrect. This type of waste does not exist in Lean.

C) Correct. This is the description of overprocessing. (Literature: A, Chapter 20.7)

D) Incorrect. This type of waste is described as creating more output then is needed and before it is needed.

18

What is the **first** step in building a customer journey map?

A) Define

B) Investigate

C) Plan

D) Research

A) Correct. This is the first step to build a customer journey map. (Literature: A, Chapter 22.7)

B) Incorrect. This is not a step in building a customer journey map.

C) Incorrect. This is a step in the Deming cycle but not in building a customer journey map.

D) Incorrect. This is the second step in building a customer journey map.

How does continuous delivery **positively** impact change control processes?

A) It does not impact the change control processes.

B) It impacts the processes through automated testing facilities.

C) It impacts the processes through delivering more information.

D) It impacts the processes through less rigorous change control.

19

Document version: v221217

A) Incorrect. Continuous delivery may positively impact change control processes by automation of the integration and testing process without human intervention or discussion.

B) Correct. Continuous delivery may impact change control process through the elimination of human intervention/human factor or discussion. (Literature: A, Chapter 23.7)

C) Incorrect. Adding more information means longer decision-making. This can negatively impact change control processes and not eliminate human errors.

D) Incorrect. A less rigorous change control process can impact more human failures and may negatively impact the whole process.

17 / 20

Technology is changing fast and this provides significant challenges for service management.

What is a generic challenge identified for service management?

A) Ensuring cost is matched to budget
B) Matching expectations to business relationships
C) More complexity and less visibility
D) Service management approaches support constraints

A) Incorrect. Ensuring cost is matched to budget is not one of the identified challenges for service management.

B) Incorrect. The challenge is to match expectations to reality, not to the relationships within the organization.

C) Correct. A recognized challenge is that emerging technologies and access to new technology can make the service provider's environment more complex. (Literature: A, Chapter 25.1)

D) Incorrect. Service management approaches need to support the organization, not the constraints.

20

What is a **key** benefit of cloud?

A) Enhanced internal communication

B) Increased quality of the infrastructure

C) Increased speed of infrastructure service

D) Reduced operating risks

A) Incorrect. Using cloud for the infrastructure will not have an impact on your ability to communicate internally. Using cloud may lead to benefits like reduced operating risks, quick provisioning of hardware and software resources, and increasing the ability to pay as you go.

B) Incorrect. Although putting infrastructure in the cloud may result in better quality, it is not a given. If there is a good internal infrastructure setup to begin with, you cannot expect an increase in quality merely by lifting it to the cloud. Using cloud may lead to benefits like reduced operating risks, quick provisioning of hardware and software resources, and increasing the ability to pay as you go.

C) Incorrect. Although you may experience higher speed of infrastructure service, this will only happen if your internal infrastructure was slow to begin with. If you have fast and efficient infrastructure service already, you cannot expect an improvement on this factor, merely by putting your infrastructure in the cloud. Using cloud may lead to benefits like reduced operating risks, quick provisioning of hardware and software resources, and increasing your ability to pay as you go.

D) Correct. The complexities of managing infrastructure servers, storage and applications is handled by the cloud provider allowing organizations to focus on core activities instead of IT technical tasks. (Literature: A, Chapter 25.2)

21

An organization decides to use a SaaS solution to control their new Internet of Things (IoT) monitoring devices.

What is **most** important to consider from a service management point of view?

A) A key requirement is that IoT devices have unique identifiers and IP addresses.

B) IoT services provide better behavior tracking to support real-time marketing.

C) It is an outsourced service, so no specific considerations are required.

D) The guardrails for the services must be respected also for SaaS solutions.

A) Incorrect. This is a valid technical requirement, but not important form a service management view.

B) Incorrect. This is a benefit that IoT services provide, but not important form a service management view.

C) Incorrect. The service management principles apply for all services.

D) Correct. The guardrails are overall principles for all services, outsourced or not. (Literature: A, Chapter 1.4 and 25.6)

An organization wants to break out of fire-fighting mode and move to the proactive mode.

On which element(s) of the VeriSM™ model should the focus be **first**?

A) Define and Produce

B) Governance

C) Management Mesh

D) Provide and Respond

22

A) Correct. Improving things from the start and producing better services is the way to go. The focus is on the Define and Produce activities, rather than repairing what went wrong. (Literature: A, Chapter 26.1)

B) Incorrect. Although these elements are important, they are not the first to focus on.

C) Incorrect. This is a necessary element for moving towards the VeriSM™ model, but does not help breaking out of the fire-fighting mode in the short term.

D) Incorrect. Focusing on what went wrong and trying to repair that, keeps the organization in fire-fight mode. The focus is on the Define and Produce activities, rather than repairing what went wrong.

23

Appendix I - Table 25 Situational Analysis of Management Practices

Table 25 Situational Analysis of Management Practices

Situational Analysis	DevOps	Agile	Lean	SIAM	CX/UX	Shift Left	Continuous Delivery
Desire to eliminate in-fighting and to break silos between development and operational teams.	X						
Desire to eliminate operational churn, defects and errors associated with deployments.	X						X
Products or services where business value needs to be obtained quickly.	X	X	X			X	
Products or services expected to incur rapid change after going live.	X	X	X			X	X
Desire to reduce manual activities involved with developing and deploying services and products.	X		X				X
Organizations looking to differentiate or uniquely promote their brand, product and services.					X	X	
Organizations looking for a strategy to keep developers closely in tune with consumer needs and how they perceive value in products and services.					X	X	
Organizations looking for a strategy to capture market share and retain customers.					X	X	
Organizations looking for innovative solutions to differentiate themselves in the marketplace.					X	X	
Organizations looking for ways in which they can significantly improve their products and services.					X	X	
Products or services where there is a need to quickly show that a specific solution or approach will either work or fail.		X					
Situations where there are concerns about meeting consumer requirements or where consumer requirements are not well understood.		X					
Desire for predictable development costs.				X			
Need to tightly control the scope of the products or services and clearly demonstrate the cost and time impact of solution changes.		X					

Appendix I - Table 25 Situational Analysis of Management Practices

Situational Analysis	DevOps	Agile	Lean	SIAM	CX/UX	Shift Left	Continuous Delivery
Providing a means to effectively manage product or service improvement.		X	X				
Products or services where the end state is not fully known.		X					
Organizations looking to effectively manage and optimize their many suppliers for better service delivery.				X			
Organizations that need to go-to-market quickly or have short timeframes for delivery of services.		X		X			
Organizations looking for a quick boost or kick-start to their supplier governance efforts.				X			
Organizations wishing to quickly access modern technologies and business solutions.		X		X	X	X	
Organizations that wish to focus on the innovation of core products and services versus the overhead of managing and coordinating many suppliers.				X			
Organizations facing a shift from a small number of suppliers to many suppliers.				X			
Desire to minimize testing risk and find integration and test errors before they become too expensive to fix.			X				X
Desire to minimize delays associated with testing efforts.			X				X
Desire to more efficiently manage and deal with services and applications that experience a high volume of change.	X	X	X			X	X
Desire to lower operating costs and increase customer satisfaction.			X		X	X	
Desire to dramatically improve and continue to improve, a service or production of a product.			X		X	X	
Desire to stop firefighting caused by problematic services and products.	X		X				
Organizations looking for ways to lower their development, deployment and operating costs.			X		X	X	